The Young Nation: America 1787-1861

Volume 1

A NEW NATION

David M. Brownstone
Irene M. Franck

GROLIER
EDUCATIONAL

About This Book

The Young Nation explores the history of the United States from the Constitution to the Civil War in 10 volumes. The first five volumes are roughly chronological, with Vol. 1 taking up American beginnings and Vol. 5 focusing strongly on slavery. The last five volumes are thematic (see the back cover for the titles).

The text of this work is supplemented throughout by boxes, sidebars, chronologies, and more than 800 full-color images, including historical paintings and photographs, plus many maps, charts, and tables specially created for this set.

Each volume includes a Master Index to the whole set. In addition, frequent cross-references in place refer readers to related sections elsewhere in the set.

Each volume also includes bibliographies of Internet sites and books for those who wish to explore that volume's topics further. More general bibliographies of Internet sites and books are provided in Vol. 10.

Also in Vol. 10 are some special materials for the period covered by the set, including:
• a table of population growth by state and territory, including breakdowns by race and by rural or urban residence;
• a list of the Presidents, including inauguration date, party, and key opponent;
• the full text of the U.S. Constitution and its first 12 Amendments;
• a Words to Know section, defining and explaining key words and concepts (which are also explained in place in the text).

Published 2002 by Grolier Educational
Old Sherman Turnpike
Danbury, Connecticut 06816

Illustration credits for all 10 volumes of *The Young Nation* are given on pp. 87–88 of Vol. 10.

Library of Congress Cataloging-in-Publication Data

Brownstone, David M.
  The young nation : America 1787-1861 / David M. Brownstone, Irene M. Franck.
    p. cm.
  Includes bibliographic references and index.
  Contents: v. 1. A new nation — v. 2. The early years — v. 3. The way West — v. 4. Beyond the Mississippi — v. 5. Slavery and the coming storm — v. 6. The new Americans — v. 7. Women's lives, women's rights — v. 8. Science, technology, and everyday life — v. 9. The arts, literature, religion, and education — v. 10. A growing nation.
  ISBN 0-7172-5645-6 (hard : set : alk. paper). —ISBN 0-7172-5646-4 (hard : v. 1 : alk. paper). —
ISBN 0-7172-5647-2 (hard : v. 2 : alk. paper). —ISBN 0-7172-5648-0 (hard : v. 3 : alk. paper). —
ISBN 0-7172-5649-9 (hard : v. 4 : alk. paper). —ISBN 0-7172-5650-2 (hard : v. 5 : alk. paper). —
ISBN 0-7172-5651-0 (hard : v. 6 : alk. paper). —ISBN 0-7172-5652-9 (hard : v. 7 : alk. paper). —
ISBN 0-7172-5653-7 (hard : v. 8 : alk. paper). —ISBN 0-7172-5654-5 (hard : v. 9 : alk. paper). —
ISBN 0-7172-5655-3 (hard : v. 10 : alk. paper).
  1. United States—History—1783-1865—Juvenile literature. [1. United States—History—1783-1865.] 1. Franck, Irene M. II. Title.

E301 .B76 2002
973—dc21   2002020047

Printed in the United States of America
Designed by K & P Publishing Services

Contents

Introduction to
The Young Nation

The Young Nation tells the story of the early history of the United States, from the signing of the Constitution in 1787 to the outbreak of the Civil War early in 1861. In the process of telling that story, we have discussed the political, social, economic, religious, scientific, technical, and cultural life of the new nation.

It took only 74 years for the new, originally weak United States to grow into a massive transcontinental power, well on its way to becoming a world power. In those years all of the main movements, ideas, and issues that would run throughout American history were brought to life—and many of them are still with us today.

In this work we have discussed the great westward movement of the American people and their nation, along with the expulsion and long retreat of the Native Americans who occupied this land before the Europeans came. We have also taken up the great underlying issue of slavery, its solution postponed during the Constitutional Convention and later again and again, while repeated secession crises threatened to destroy the Union. Ultimately, the joined issues of slavery and secession would be resolved, but only by the Civil War.

We have here also taken up the long and continuing struggle for American democracy, won in the American Revolution, set out in the Declaration of Independence, Constitution, and Bill of Rights, and expanded during the first seven decades of our history. The antislavery and women's rights movements, the Alien and Sedition Acts, and many reform movements all figure heavily in early American history.

We have also discussed the massive surge of immigration that began in the 1840s, especially as it combined with the great westward movement and the rise of the American factory system. All of these brought enormous changes to American life.

Framing it all, we have throughout placed the new United States in the much wider world of which it was a part.

David M. Brownstone
Irene M. Franck

If You Had Been Born in 1790

Many of the people who settled the heartland of North America and then moved on all the way to the Pacific had originally come from the East Coast colonies. This family was settling in Ohio when it was still part of the frontier. But many like them later moved on farther west.

If you had been born in 1790, and lived until what was then the ripe old age of 70, then this story of the early years of the new United States would be the story of your life and times.

How your life went would have depended partly on who you were. As it turned out, if you were a White American born in 1790, you would by 1860 be a citizen of a huge country that

Right from the start, in many parts of the country the lives of the rich and poor were very far apart. Poorest of all were those who were enslaved. Slaveholders included some of the founders of the United States, such as George Washington (second from right), painted as a Virginia plantation owner by Junius Brutus Stearns in about 1853.

stretched from the Atlantic to the Pacific, and from the Gulf of Mexico to the Canadian border. In the process of becoming that country, the United States would take vast Native-American lands and half of Mexico. It would also acquire a big piece of the disputed Pacific Northwest from Britain.

You might have lived your whole life no more than a few miles from home, in one of the 13 original East Coast states, which were British colonies before the American Revolution. Or, like so many others, you could have gone west at any time in your life.

You might have followed Daniel Boone across the Appalachian Mountains through Cumberland Gap into Kentucky. Or you might have traveled north up the Hudson River and west on the Mohawk Trail, or south around the mountains through Georgia. Later you could have gone farther west, to Texas and beyond. There you would have fought and won the two wars that took the United States all the way to the Pacific. Or you might have joined a wagon train west on the Oregon Trail, perhaps to mine gold in California during the gold rush days, or to take Native-American lands and settle in the Pacific Northwest.

On the other hand, you might have been an African American born into slavery in 1790. At that time, almost one out of four Americans were African Americans, and most of them were slaves. Then your life would most probably have been hard, short, and brutal, as were the lives of most victims of the great crime of slavery. You might have been one of the few slaves who escaped to freedom, sometimes with the help of abolitionists on the Underground Railroad. Or you might have been one of those who became free when slavery was abolished in many northern states. For the great majority of African-American slaves, freedom would not come in their lifetimes. It would come only with Union victory in the Civil War.

Or you might have been born a Native American in 1790. If you were born in the original United States, you would most likely have been pushed westward by the invading Americans again and again during your lifetime. In the process, you would lose most of the lands that had been your birthright. You would have seen your soldiers defeated by invading U.S. forces, and many Native-American peoples destroyed as their lands were taken by White American settlers.

If you had been born and lived in Spanish-controlled northern Mexico in 1790, you would have seen two major wars in your lifetime. The first would be the Mexican Revolution, which won Mexico's independence from Spain, as the American Revolution had won independence from Britain. The second war, however, would end with the loss of half of Mexico to the United States. Then your later years might have been lived as part of a conquered and often abused people.

The lives of Comanche children like these would be utterly changed by the westward push of the Americans. Most Native-American peoples would be forced out of their homelands and onto reservations.

8

American Beginnings

The story of the new United States is part of a much longer story—that of the European invasion and conquest of the Americas. In some ways, it is even bigger and wider than that. The taking of the Americas was only part of a period when Europeans conquered much of the whole world.

In the spring of 1453, after centuries of Muslim-Christian warfare in the Middle East, the forces of the expanding Ottoman-Turkish empire finally took Constantinople (earlier Byzantium, later Istanbul). The massive old city, originally Greek, linked the Mediterranean and Black Seas. By then it had been the greatest of East-West gateways for 2,000 years.

The Ottoman Turks, who were Muslims, were in the process of taking much of southern and eastern Europe from their Christian opponents. They shut that East-West gateway. With that they cut Europe's main trade routes to the much-prized spices,

gems, woods, artworks, and other products of the great civilizations of the East.

European attention then focused on finding new ways of reaching the East. The Portuguese, who had been inching their way south along the African coast since the early 1400s, stepped up their efforts. In the 1440s they began taking Black Africans back to Portugal as slaves. This was the beginning of the Atlantic slave trade. (Though Africans of other races would sometimes be enslaved, the first slaves taken to Portugal and those taken to North America were Black Africans.) Portuguese sailor Vasco da Gama rounded the Cape of Good Hope in 1497 and reached India in the spring of 1498. By 1502, using their superior firepower, Portuguese forces had started the long series of attacks that would give them control of much of the Indian Ocean—until the other European powers caught up.

Atlantic Crossings

Portugal—and Spain—also turned west. On August 3, 1492, Italian navigator Christopher Columbus (born Cristoforo Colombo) led a flotilla of three Spanish ships, the *Niña*, *Pinta*, and *Santa María*, west across the Atlantic out of Palos, Spain. Embracing the idea that the Earth was round, he sought to reach

This is the earliest known picture of Columbus and his ships landing in the New World. The woodcut is from the Narrative of Columbus, *a poem by Giuliano Dati, published in Florence, Italy, in 1493, a year after that historic event.*

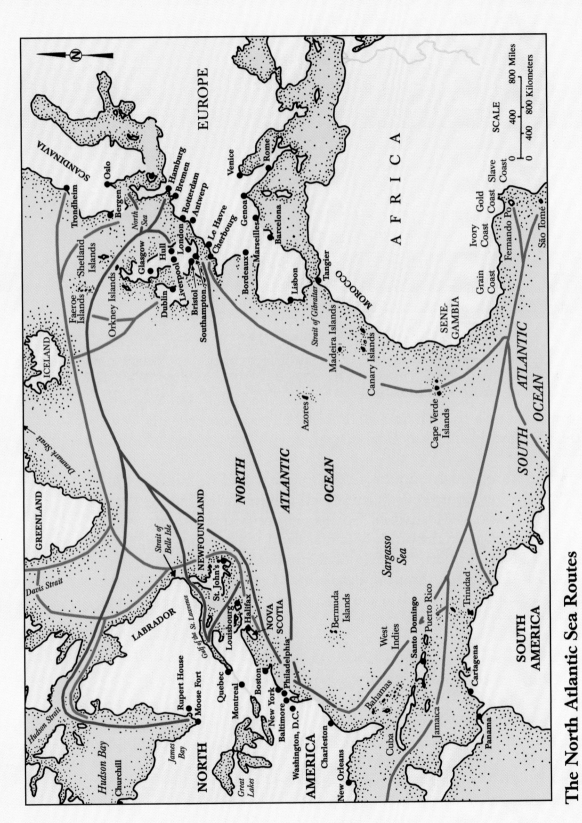

The North Atlantic Sea Routes

—— Early Exploratory Routes

—— Later Main Sailing Routes

—— Main Slave Trade Routes

Before the arrival of the Europeans, the Native-American peoples had many distinct cultures. Some lived in large towns, which the Spanish would call pueblos, *like this one in Mesa Verde. A modern artist shows priests emerging by ladder (center) from the sacred underground religious chamber, or* kiva.

the Spice Islands of the East Indies. He had no idea as to how far away they really were. Instead he reached the Caribbean Sea, making his first landing in the New World on October 12, 1492, on an island he called San Salvador, in what is now the Bahamas. He returned to Spain in early 1493, taking some Native-American captives with him, a sign of things to come.

The European conquest of the Americas had begun. By 1500 Portuguese explorer Pedro Cabral had claimed what is now Brazil for his country. Meanwhile Spanish-sponsored explorers made huge territorial claims on the mainlands of the continents that we now call North America and South America. Spain went on to conquer Mexico's Aztec Empire, Peru's Inca Empire, and then all the rest of Central America, the Caribbean, and South America, except for Brazil.

Slavery and Conquest

With the beginning of the European conquest of the Americas came the beginning of slavery. In 1501 the first Black Africans were brought as slaves to the New World, to the Caribbean island of Hispaniola (today shared by Haiti and the Dominican Republic). Before the Atlantic slave trade ended in 1870, an estimated 9.6 million to 11.5 million African slaves would be brought to the Americas. At least two million more Africans died on slave ships coming across the Atlantic during that period (see Vol. 5, p. 7).

The European conquest also brought the beginning of a four-centuries-long series of European attacks on Native-American peoples. Many Caribbean peoples were enslaved and destroyed by the invaders. (African slaves were imported to replace them.)

On the mainlands of Central and South America, many Native-American peoples were largely destroyed by diseases carried by the Europeans. They had never been exposed to many diseases new to the Americas, so they had no immunity (built-in resistance) against them. The same thing would also happen to many Native Americans in North America.

Slavery in the New World began in the Caribbean in 1501. This fort at Christiansted guarded one of the Caribbean's largest slave markets, on the island Columbus named Santa Cruz, now called St. Croix Island, part of the U.S. Virgin Islands.

The Conquest

Before the Europeans arrived, the Native Americans did not have horses to ride or carry their gear. Instead, they packed their goods in backpacks or on a travois, a frame on two poles, with one end tied to a dog and the other trailing on the ground, as in this painting of Kiowa traveling on the prairie.

The European conquest of the regions that would become the United States began only about 500 years ago. That is a short time when compared with the history of humanity in the Americas.

People from Asia, the ancestors of the Native Americans, began arriving at least 13,000 years ago. They came across what was then a land bridge from Siberia to Alaska. Some may have come much earlier, possibly as early as 50,000–70,000 years ago. By the time the European conquerors came in the early 1500s, an estimated one million to three million Native Americans of many cultures lived in what is now the United States.

After the Native Americans, the first people to come to the North American mainland and stay permanently were the Europeans of the 1500s. Some other visitors from Africa and Asia may have arrived centuries earlier, but there is no conclusive proof that they did so. There is hard proof that Greenland was settled by Norse rovers led by Erik the Red in the 980s, and that the Norse also settled on the Newfoundland coast in the centuries that followed.

Some Norse settlements in Greenland probably lasted until the early 1400s, less than a century before the European conquerors came to the Americas, but those settlements did not survive the "Little Ice

Age." This was a period of much colder than normal weather, when the sea lanes of the North Atlantic were clogged with ice for much of the year.

Invaders Who Stayed

However, the invading Europeans of the 1500s came to North America, stayed, and conquered. In what would become the United States, the result was centuries of epidemic diseases, "Indian Wars," and "Indian Removals." These destroyed most Native-American cultures and the vast majority of Native Americans.

At the same time, the invasion meant centuries of conflict among the European nations themselves. This was part of a global set of conflicts over the "spoils" of the whole world. Britain, France, Spain, the Netherlands, Sweden, and Russia were the main contenders for the rich lands of North America. In the end, the new United States emerged. It took by far the most valuable, resource-rich, and fertile parts of North America. Canada and Mexico would develop as independent nations holding the rest of the continent.

European explorers had reached the North American mainland in the late 1400s. The first was John Cabot (really an Italian sailor born Giovanni Caboto). He headed an English expedition that explored the Newfoundland coast and possibly farther south in 1497. In the same period, possibly even before the Cabot voyage, British, Portuguese, Basque, and Breton sailors were fishing the rich Grand Banks off Newfoundland, drying their cod on shore, and trading with Native Americans.

Many European explorers followed Cabot. Juan Ponce de León reached Florida in 1513, claiming it for Spain. Giovanni da Verrazano, another Italian leading an English expedition, explored the northern Atlantic coast in 1524. French seafarer Jacques Cartier reached Canada's Gulf of St. Lawrence in 1534.

The first thing that colonists had to do when they arrived was to build shelters. These settlers, who arrived by water, are putting up a log cabin on the shore.

On their 1540 expedition into the American Southwest, Coronado and his soldiers, called conquistadores, took Zuni Pueblo (Zuni City), a scene painted here by a modern artist.

The Spanish Colonies

Spain was the first of the European colonial nations to establish and hold European settlements in what would become the United States. With the Spanish settlements the European conquest of North America began. From 1539 to 1541, Hernando de Soto's expedition traveled from Florida all the way to the Mississippi River.

The arrival of the Spanish triggered huge epidemics that killed large numbers of Native-American peoples. The problem was that Native Americans had never been exposed to many of the diseases the Europeans carried, so they had built up no resistance to those diseases.

In 1540 Francisco Vásquez de Coronado traveled north out of Mexico, reaching the Grand Canyon. On the way he captured the Zuni Pueblo (Zuni City) in a major attack on the Pueblo peoples of the Southwest. That began the long "Indian Wars" in the American Southwest. Coronado brought the horse to North America, which would transform the lives of the Native Americans of the Great Plains.

Spanish seafarers reached the Pacific coast in 1542. That was when Juan Cabrillo's two ships entered San Diego Bay. They started from Navidad, near modern Acapulco, Mexico, and explored the coast all the way to Oregon.

French forces established Florida's Fort Caroline in 1564, but they were defeated by the Spanish a year later. In 1565 Spain

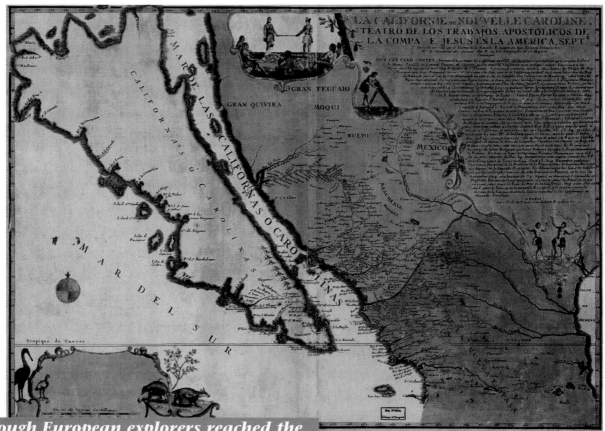

Though European explorers reached the Pacific coast in the mid-1500s, for a long time they knew little about the lands in that area. California was thought to be an island, as it appears on this map published by N. de Fer in Paris in 1720.

California as an Island

established a small settlement at St. Augustine, Florida. That became the first permanent Spanish (and European) settlement in what is now the United States. Spanish settlement of Florida came slowly, however. The Spanish did not move in and take full possession of Florida until Pensacola was established in 1698.

The first major Spanish settlement in the United States came in 1598. That was when Don Juan de Oñate founded the new Mexican province of Nuevo (New) Mexico. He led a party of 200 Spanish colonists north out of central Mexico on El Camino Real (The Royal Road) to reach the Rio Grande (Big River, in Mexico the Río Bravo) at El Paso (The Pass) and then settle in the new province. Its capital, founded in 1610, was Santa Fe (Holy Faith). In 1848, after the Mexican-American War, that whole territory would be taken by the United States, along with the rest of the American Southwest and California (see Vol. 4, pp. 20–34).

Mission San Diego de Alcala was founded in 1769 by Father Junípero Serra, a Franciscan missionary. It was the first of a string of missions in what is now called the California Mission Trail.

Spain did not establish permanent settlements in California until more than a century and a half later, starting in the late 1760s. In 1769 Franciscan missionary Junípero Serra and Captain Gaspar de Portolá established the Mission San Diego de Alcala, which gave its name to modern San Diego. In the same period the Spanish established a land route from Santa Fe to California.

The San Diego Mission was the first of a string of 21 California missions established over the next 54 years on what is now called the California Mission Trail. Yet even with the missions in place, Spanish emigration to California was small. In 1790

California had fewer than 1,000 Spanish residents, including priests, soldiers, and colonists.

With Spanish rule came the extraordinarily fast destruction of California's Native-American population. As elsewhere, the Spanish brought epidemic diseases with them. The missions also brought with them very real slavery, though the Spanish called it religious conversion and employment. Between the mid-1700s and the early 1800s, California's Native-American population fell dramatically, from an estimated 300,000 to an estimated 200,000 (see Vol. 4, p. 85).

The French Colonies

The Appalachian mountain chain stretches from Georgia all the way into the Canadian North. For Europeans reaching the Americas from northern Europe, the best way into North America by far is the northern route opened up by French sea captain Jacques Cartier in 1534.

After sailing across the North Atlantic, Cartier discovered the Strait of Belle Isle, between the northern tip of Newfoundland and the Quebec mainland. He then sailed into the Gulf of St. Lawrence, the great gateway to the St. Lawrence River and all of North America.

A year later, in 1535, Cartier came back. This time he entered the St. Lawrence River and sailed all the way up the river to the Native-American villages that would become the sites of Quebec City and Montreal. His ocean-going ship could not go beyond the Lichine Rapids, near Montreal. However, that was quite far enough, for at Montreal he was west of the Appalachians, and North America was wide open for the French.

Cartier opened up the main northern route into the North American heartland. The St. Lawrence is a great natural water route that goes directly from the sea right through the Appalachians. Very early, French explorers and fur traders followed it to the great inland seas called the Great

19

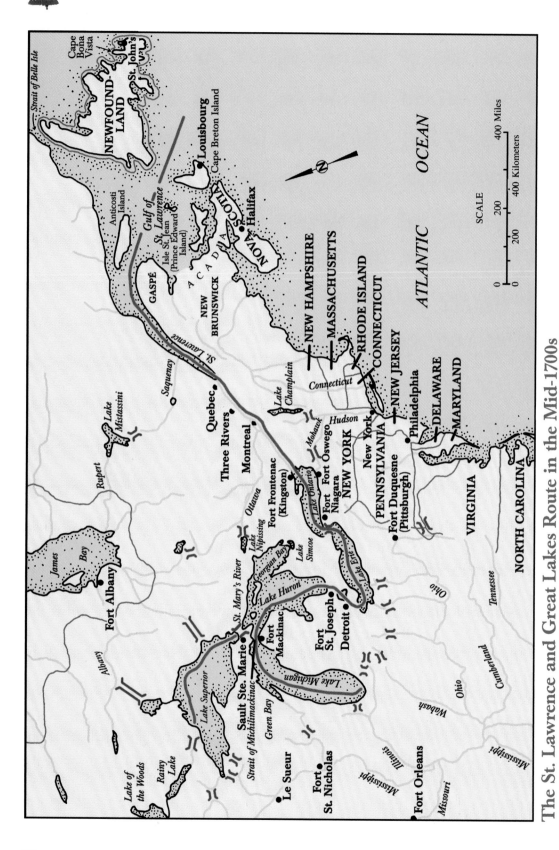

The St. Lawrence and Great Lakes Route in the Mid-1700s

— Main St. Lawrence–Great Lakes Route

—— Boundaries of English Settlements

)(Main Portages

Note: Portages are places where early travelers had to carry (*portage* in French) or drag their canoes or boats overland from one waterway to another.

Catholic missionaries often joined early French explorers, like this Jesuit missionary preaching to Native Americans and traders.

Lakes, going far out into the Midwest through Lake Michigan and Lake Superior, there linking up with the huge Mississippi-Missouri river basin. (In modern times this route from the western end of the Great Lakes through the St. Lawrence River to the sea would become the St. Lawrence Seaway.)

Piercing the mountain chain, French explorers, traders, and settlers—along with Catholic missionaries—built what would become an American empire that reached as far as the mouth of the Mississippi River to the south and the Rocky Mountains to the west. The French did this all while the English were still confined to their East Coast colonies.

Samuel de Champlain founded France's first permanent North American colony in 1605, at The Habitation at Port Royal in New France (later Annapolis, Nova Scotia). In 1608 he founded Quebec City, and by 1615 he had explored deep into mid-continent, as far as Lake Huron. He was followed by many other French explorers, trappers, and traders. Among them was Daniel Duluth, who in 1678 explored the western end of Lake Superior. In 1679 Robert Cavelier de La Salle explored the Mississippi River all the way to the Gulf of Mexico. Other explorers would take the French all the way to the Rockies.

It was this French empire that Britain would take at the end of the long British-French struggle for North America. After the American Revolution, the new American nation would win from Britain a huge part of that empire, from Canada to Spanish-held Mexico and out to the Mississippi. In 1803 the Americans would buy from France a great deal more of the original French empire, from the Mississippi to the Rockies, in the Louisiana Purchase (see Vol. 2, p. 58). However, Britain still held Canada. The Americans would have to go around and through the Appalachians without using the Canadian route (see Vol. 3, p. 14).

This image is called **The First Day at Jamestown.** *It shows workers cutting up wood to use in building shelters, while the expedition's aristocratic leaders stand or sit at their leisure.*

The British Colonies

The British colonies in North America were founded later than those of the French and Spanish, but they became the most powerful of all. From them grew the United States.

The first successful British North American settlement was founded in 1607 at Jamestown, Virginia. With that colony came several major developments—the beginning of centuries of "Indian Wars" between the British (later Americans) and the Native Americans; the beginning of

African slavery in the British colonies and then the United States; and the widespread cultivation of tobacco. That crop would become the early basis of the southern plantation system, which would foster slavery.

The first 20 Black Africans to enter England's North American colonies were brought against their will as slaves to Jamestown in 1619. These first African Americans would be followed by an estimated 400,000 to 500,000 African slaves, brought into what is now the United States between then and the Emancipation Proclamation in 1863 (see Vol. 5, p. 7). Their presence as forced labor made possible the southern plantation system, especially in the cultivation of tobacco and later cotton.

The East Coast Indian Wars also began at Jamestown. In 1609 minor skirmishing began between the Jamestown colonists and the Native Americans of the Powhatan Confederacy, on whose lands the colonists had settled. Open war flared in 1622, with a Powhatan massacre of British settlers, which was followed by 14 years of Powhatan-British war. By the early 1660s, the Powhatans had been destroyed. The few survivors fled before the advancing tide of British settlement. It was a pattern that would be repeated for almost three centuries, from the Atlantic to the Pacific.

Today Pocahontas, a Powhatan princess, is probably the most famous of the Native Americans who lived in what is now Virginia. She is credited with saving the life of Captain John Smith in 1607, though she herself was later taken hostage by the British. She married British colonist John Rolfe in 1614. They and their young son went to Britain two years later, where she was presented to King James I, but she died on the eve of their return. This modern painting is based on a 1616 portrait made before she "renounced idolatree"—that is, converted to Christianity.

The East Coast Colonies Grow

In 1620 a group of Puritans arrived on the *Mayflower* and founded the Plymouth Colony in what is now Massachusetts. They were Dissenters—that is, they disagreed with the main Anglican religion in Britain—who called themselves Pilgrims. In the years that followed, they were joined by tens of thousands of other British Puritans. They founded the powerful Massachusetts Bay colony and the other New England colonies, which would become states after the American Revolution.

European immigrants from many countries, as well as Black Africans brought as slaves, settled on the East Coast of North America. In 1612 the Dutch founded their New Netherlands colony, centered on the Hudson Valley, establishing Fort Nassau (Albany) in 1614, and New Amsterdam (New York) in 1626. At that time, the Netherlands was a great European power, beginning its conquest of the East Indies (now Indonesia), as well as founding colonies in the Americas.

One of the key figures in the colony of Pennsylvania was British Quaker leader William Penn. In this painting by Benjamin West, he is shown making a 1683 peace treaty with Native Americans in Philadelphia.

Sweden, another great European power then, established an American colony in 1638, centered on Fort Christina (now Wilmington), on the Delaware River. The Dutch took it in 1655. However, the British won it 1674, along with the whole New Netherlands colony, after winning a worldwide British-Dutch war.

Early immigrants from many countries poured into the British East Coast colonies during the colonial period. Many of those counted as British were Scottish and Welsh. From Ireland came both Catholics and Protestants, many of them recently involved in what would become four centuries of Catholic-Protestant conflict in Northern Ireland. Large numbers of Scotch-Irish and Welsh settlers went directly out to the colonial frontier. There they would become part of the long American drive west, which would finally take them to the Pacific.

A good many early immigrants had been religious and political dissenters and refugees in Europe. From France came thousands of Protestant Huguenots, fleeing from the massacres generated by the Catholic-Protestant religious wars of the period. Starting in 1683, groups of persecuted German Protestants began arriving in Pennsylvania and neighboring colonies, among them Mennonites and Quakers. Many called themselves "Deutsch," meaning German, so they came to be called "Pennsylvania Dutch."

By 1700 Britain had gained a strong foothold in North America. Its East Coast colonies stretched from New Hampshire in the north to Virginia in the south, and farther south included Charleston, South Carolina. Settlers were beginning to move inland, though they largely stayed east of the Appalachian Mountains.

By this time the British colonial population numbered an estimated 251,000 people, including almost 28,000 African Americans, most of them slaves. Tens of thousands of Native Americans still lived in the British colonies as well, though substantial numbers had by then been killed by epidemic diseases, or had been driven north, south, and west by the colonists. However, no good estimate is available of the total number of Native Americans left in the British areas of settlement.

Early European colonists crossed the Atlantic in small ships like this one. Called the **Mayflower II,** *it is a replica of the ship that brought the first Pilgrims to America.*

A New People

These are the streets of New York City on the morning of April 30, 1789, as George Washington (center) rode to Federal Hall, where he would become the first President of the United States.

During the 1700s something new began to happen in British colonial America: Many European Americans in the British colonies began to see themselves as a single people, to form themselves into a new nation. Colonial populations and trade grew enormously, and ties between what had been separate colonies grew as well.

Britain's North American colonies grew rapidly during the 1700s. Between 1700 and 1750 the population of the colonies grew by almost five times, to more than 1,170,000. More than 236,000 of these were African Americans, most of them slaves. By 1770, six years before the American Revolution, the colonial population had nearly doubled again, to almost 2,150,000, including 460,000 African Americans.

A good deal of this massive growth was due to "natural increase"—that is, to growth resulting from more births than deaths. However, much of the growth was also due to sharply increasing immigration from Europe, along with the arrival of large numbers of newly kidnapped and enslaved Africans.

Growth of Population in the 13 British-American Colonies, 1610–1780

	Total Population	Total European-American Population	Percentage of European Americans in Total Population	Total African-American Population	Percentage of African Americans in Total Population
1610	350	350	100.00	0	0.00
1620	2,302	2,282	99.13	20	0.87
1630	4,646	4,586	98.71	60	1.29
1640	26,634	26,037	97.76	597	2.24
1650	50,368	48,768	96.82	1,600	2.24
1660	75,058	72,138	96.11	2,920	3.18
1670	111,935	107,400	95.95	4,535	4.05
1680	151,507	144,536	95.40	6,971	4.60
1690	210,371	193,642	92.05	16,729	7.95
1700	250,888	223,071	88.91	27,817	11.09
1710	331,711	286,845	86.47	44,866	13.53
1720	466,185	397,346	85.23	68,839	14.77
1730	629,445	538,424	85.54	91,021	14.46
1740	905,563	755,539	83.43	150,024	16.57
1750	1,170,760	934,340	79.81	236,420	20.19
1760	1,593,625	1,267,819	79.56	325,806	20.44
1770	2,148,076	1,688,254	78.59	459,822	21.41
1780	2,780,369	2,204,949	79.30	575,420	20.70

Note: The figures used in this table are estimates of the European-American and African-American populations of the 13 English colonies that would become the United States. Native-American populations were not estimated. The table is adapted from a table in *Historical Statistics of the United States*, Bicentennial Edition, U.S. Bureau of the Census, 1975, Chapter C 89–119.

The areas of British settlement also increased greatly. By the mid-1700s, an almost uninterrupted strip of British colonies stretched from northern Maine to southern Georgia, and inland into the eastern Appalachians.

During the long British-French battle for North America, both sides had Native-American allies. British colonial policy therefore made it difficult for American settlers to freely move west, beyond the Appalachians.

Even so, some American settlers pushed through the mountains before the American Revolution. They moved into the eastern end of the Mohawk Valley, through the mountains in central Pennsylvania, and around the southern end of the mountain chain in Georgia. They also moved into Kentucky through the mountain pass called Cumberland Gap. There in

March 1775 Daniel Boone and 30 axemen cleared the Wilderness Road (see Vol. 3, p. 20), which would become a gateway used by millions of Americans going west into the heart of the continent.

The great majority of Americans were farmers then, as would continue to be true after the Revolution. What most of all drew them west was the prospect of good, inexpensive land, which meant taking land that had long belonged to Native Americans. That taking was done by force or the threat of force, though it was often described as a "purchase" of the land from the Native Americans. Land speculators—individuals and groups of moneyed Europeans and Americans—acquired huge blocks of territory and then resold it to smaller speculators and to farmers who settled the land.

The earliest routes through the Appalachian Mountains were little more than footpaths through the woods, like that shown here preserved in the Levi Jackson Wilderness Road State Park in Kentucky.

Whatever the technique used, the Native Americans who had held the land were driven out, often violently. Their homes were abandoned and destroyed and their cultures destroyed as well. Many of the leading citizens of the colonies held large blocks of wilderness land and profited handsomely as great masses of Americans moved west. That would be so throughout the history of the westward-moving frontier.

Daniel Boone and his axemen were an example of how it worked. In the spring of 1775, land speculator Thomas Henderson and his assistant, Daniel Boone, met with the leaders of the Cherokee Nation. For only a few thousand pounds, they "bought" for the Pennsylvania Land Company a right of way through Cumberland Gap and an estimated 20 million acres of land on the other side of the Gap. Dragging Canoe, a son of one of the Cherokee chiefs, later told Boone: "You have bought a fair land, but there is a cloud hanging over it. You will find its settlement dark and bloody."

And so it was, for the Cherokees had "sold" lands that were not theirs to sell. The lands were also claimed by the Shawnees and other Native-American nations. Boone and his men were attacked by the Shawnees as soon as they came through the Gap. That began a series of "Indian Wars" that would finally result in the defeat and expulsion of all the Native-American peoples from their homelands in the region.

American trade and industry also grew fast during the 1700s. As the colonies grew, Americans began to build the economy that would one day make the United States a major world power. Homegrown industries began to supply American needs.

I undertook to mark out a road in the best passage from the settlement through the wilderness to Kentucke. . . .We proceeded with all possible expedition until we came within fifteen miles of where Boonsborough now stands, and there we were fired upon by a party of Indians that killed two, and wounded two of our number. . . This was on the 20th of March, 1775. Three days after that we were fired upon again, and had two men killed, and three wounded. Afterwards we proceeded on to Kentucky river without opposition; and on the first day of April began to erect the fort of Boonsborough. . . .

DANIEL BOONE DESCRIBING THE BUILDING OF BOONESBOROUGH, KENTUCKY

As settlers moved into Native-American lands, they were often met with resistance and violence. To settlers, that was reason enough to try to push the Native Americans westward. This image from Humphry Marshall's History of Kentucky *(1812) shows an attack on Daniel and Squire Boone, who survived, and John Stewart, who was killed.*

New England's ships went into the rich West Indies trade. Its whalers and fishers, along with its grim and bloody slavers, created a strong maritime industry. New York and Pennsylvania became the "breadbasket" of the fast-expanding colonies, and the southern plantation system grew highly profitable tobacco for export.

On the western frontier the fur trade also became a major industry. Trappers and traders were in the process of destroying the beaver and other fur-bearing animals they would pursue all the way to the Pacific.

American colonists gained crucial military experience fighting alongside the British against the French. Among them was a young George Washington, shown here planting the British flag at France's Fort Duquesne, which became Britain's Fort Pitt and later Pittsburgh, Pennsylvania.

France against Britain

American colonists began to share the experience of war as well. During the 1700s a key fact of American life was that Britain, France, and other European powers were engaged in a long series of wars over which nations would win the battle for world empire—of course, at the expense of the peoples they conquered.

In North America that battle for world empire expressed itself as a series of British-French wars. The most notable of these was the French and Indian War (1754–1763), which was part of the worldwide Seven Years War (1756–1763). Colonial troops joined British and French armies and fleets in these conflicts. In the process, the Americans and their officers gained military experience that would prepare them for the American Revolution.

One force of American troops during the French and Indian War was commanded by a then-young American officer named George Washington. He and his forces were captured by the French in 1754. They were defeated again with British general Edward Braddock in 1755. Twenty years later, in 1775, Washington would take command of the Continental Army. He would lead it to victory in the American Revolution, going on to become the first American President and "the father of his country."

The British won the Seven Years War. With that victory the long British-French battle for North America ended. At the end, in 1763, Britain held all of Canada and almost all of what would become the United States, all the way from the Atlantic to the Mississippi River. Only 12 years later, in 1775, the British and colonial American troops who had fought side by side against France would go to war again—this time against each other.

Early Americans joined British redcoats in fighting against the French in the French and Indian War. Marching on a narrow trail through the forests, General Edward Braddock's forces were headed for France's Fort Duquesne (later Pittsburgh, Pennsylvania).

Toward Revolution

The set of problems that generated the American Revolution grew quickly during the 1700s. One major problem was that the vast majority of American international trade was with Britain, the home country. This was not a matter of choice. Rather, it was forced on the colonies by British law. That required unequal trade, which favored British merchants and investors over Americans.

The direct run-up to the American Revolution began after 1763, at the end of the Seven Years War (French and Indian War). Faced with huge war debts, Britain passed the Sugar Act, which imposed heavy new taxes on the American colonies. Its Currency Act barred the colonies from issuing their own money. The 1765 Stamp Act brought still more heavy new taxes. The Townshend Acts brought yet another body of new taxes in 1767.

American colonial governments and

popular groups such as the Sons of Liberty organized determined resistance. They forced repeal of some of the taxes, but others remained, most notably the tax on tea.

The conflict grew. In 1770 five protesting Americans were killed by British troops in Boston, in the Boston Massacre. At the "Boston Tea Party" in 1773, Boston citizens dumped British tea into Boston harbor in protest against the new Tea Act.

The British government answered with a series of Coercive Acts. These included closing the Port of Boston and forcing Americans to quarter British troops in their homes.

Americans responded with even better organized resistance, meanwhile arming themselves for war. That came on April 19, 1775, when the American militia defeated British regulars at Lexington and Concord, in Massachusetts, and then laid siege to British-occupied Boston.

American colonists were far from united going into the Revolution. Large numbers of the "best people" were Loyalists. They regarded themselves as steadfastly British

Under an old elm tree in Cambridge, Massachusetts, George Washington is shown taking command of the American army.

Concord Hymn

By the rude bridge that arched the flood,
Their flag to April's breeze unfurled,
Here once the embattled farmers stood,
And fired the shot heard round the world.

The foe long since in silence slept;
Alike the conqueror sleeps;
And Time the ruined bridge has swept
Down the dark stream that seaward creeps.

On this green bank, by this soft stream,
We set today a votive stone;
That memory may their deed redeem,
When, like our sires, our sons are gone.

Spirit that made these heroes dare
To die, or leave their children free,
Bid Time and Nature gently spare
The shaft we raise to them and thee.

THIS POEM BY RALPH WALDO EMERSON WAS SUNG AS A HYMN AT A CEREMONY ON APRIL 19, 1836, DEDICATING A MONUMENT AT CONCORD, MASSACHUSETTS, TO THE AMERICAN REVOLUTIONARIES.

Near this little bridge at Concord, Massachusetts, stands the Minute Man Statue (behind flag). Like these modern soldiers in period uniform, the statue honors the early revolutionaries of the area, who called themselves Minute Men.

Before radio and television, and before most people could read, important documents were often read out loud to the public. This image shows the first public reading of the Declaration of Independence, by John Nixon, a member of the Philadelphia Committee of Safety, from the steps of Independence Hall.

and had no intention of joining the revolutionaries. Many Loyalists fought with British forces during the war. At war's end, most would leave the country with the British, settling in Canada, Britain, and other British-held areas.

Nor were the revolutionaries themselves united on many key matters. They had very serious disagreements on major matters. This included the basic question of whether to create a fully formed central government (a *federation*) or a group of loosely allied former colonies operating as largely independent small countries (a *confederation*). Underneath, too, was the basic question of slavery, which would underlie all of early American history and lead to the Civil War.

> *We must all hang together, or assuredly we shall all hang separately.*
>
> BENJAMIN FRANKLIN, AT THE SIGNING OF THE DECLARATION OF INDEPENDENCE, JULY 4, 1776.

On July 4, 1776, a little more than a year after the Revolution began, the Second Continental Congress, meeting at Philadelphia, adopted the Declaration of Independence (see p. 38). Written by Thomas Jefferson, it was a landmark in the history of human freedom, and was also the final American break with Britain.

The Declaration of Independence

IN CONGRESS, July 4, 1776. The unanimous Declaration of the Thirteen United States of America,

When in the Course of human events, it becomes necessary for one people to dissolve the political bands which have connected them with another, and to assume among the Powers of the earth, the separate and equal station to which the Laws of Nature and of Nature's God entitle them, a decent respect to the opinions of mankind requires that they should declare the causes which impel them to the separation.

We hold these truths to be self-evident, that all men are created equal, that they are endowed by their Creator with certain unalienable Rights, that among these are Life, Liberty and the pursuit of Happiness. That to secure these rights, Governments are instituted among Men, deriving their just powers from the consent of the governed, That whenever any Form of Government becomes destructive of these ends, it is the Right of the People to alter or to abolish it, and to institute new Government, laying its foundation on such principles and organizing its powers in such form, as to them shall seem most likely to effect their Safety and Happiness. Prudence, indeed, will dictate that Governments long established should not be changed for light and transient causes; and accordingly all experience hath shown, that mankind are more disposed to suffer, while evils are sufferable, than to right themselves by abolishing the forms to which they are accustomed. But when a long train of abuses and usurpations, pursuing invariably the same Object evinces a design to reduce them under absolute Despotism, it is their right, it is their duty, to throw off such Government, and to provide new Guards for their future security.—Such has been the patient sufferance of these Colonies; and such is now the necessity which constrains them to alter their former Systems of Government. . . . [There followed a list of specific grievances against Britain.]

We, therefore, the Representatives of the United States of America, in General Congress, Assembled, appealing to the Supreme Judge of the world for the rectitude of our intentions, do, in the Name, and by Authority of the good People of these Colonies, solemnly publish and declare, That these United Colonies are, and of Right ought to be Free and Independent States; that they are Absolved from all Allegiance to the British Crown, and that all political connection between them and the State of Great Britain, is and ought to be totally dissolved; and that as Free and Independent States, they have full Power to levy War, conclude Peace, contract Alliances, establish Commerce, and to do all other Acts and Things which Independent States may of right do. And for the support of this Declaration, with a firm reliance on the protection of divine Providence, we mutually pledge to each other our Lives, our Fortunes and our sacred Honor.

The author of the Declaration of Independence was Thomas Jefferson. The American ambassador to France in the mid-1780s, he would later serve as the first U.S. Secretary of State, as Vice President, and then as the third President of the United States.

Winning the Revolution

It took eight years of war to win American independence. Following Lexington and Concord, the Americans forced the British to leave Boston in March 1776. However, a British army commanded by William Howe came in from the sea to defeat George Washington's American forces and take New York City. Howe's forces went on to take Philadelphia and most of New Jersey during the rest of the year. The remnants of the American army spent the winter at Valley Forge, Pennsylvania, and the American cause seemed very close to lost.

A major turn occurred in the summer and autumn of 1777: At Saratoga, New York, American forces surrounded a British

Emanuel Leutze's painting **Washington Crossing the Delaware,** *a scene during the Revolution, was so popular that many copies of it were made. Leutze himself commissioned this 1851 copy by his pupil Eastman Johnson, who would also become a noted artist.*

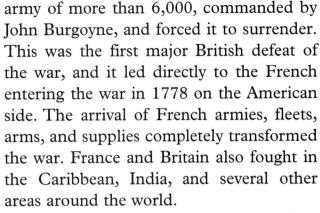

army of more than 6,000, commanded by John Burgoyne, and forced it to surrender. This was the first major British defeat of the war, and it led directly to the French entering the war in 1778 on the American side. The arrival of French armies, fleets, arms, and supplies completely transformed the war. France and Britain also fought in the Caribbean, India, and several other areas around the world.

In 1779 Spain also went to war against Britain. Spanish forces quickly took control of the lower Mississippi River. They cleared British troops and warships from the area and stopped a threatened British invasion of New Orleans. In 1780 Spanish forces took Mobile, in what is now Alabama. The following year a 7,000-strong Spanish army

Some women were frontline soldiers in the American Revolution. Here is Molly Pitcher (Mary Ludwig Hays), who took the place of her dead husband at a cannon in the battle of Monmouth, New Jersey, in 1778.

41

besieged and took heavily fortified Fort St. George at Pensacola, Florida.

The final and decisive major battle of the American Revolution came in the autumn of 1781 at Yorktown, Virginia. There combined American and French forces numbering 15,000, led by George Washington and Jean Baptiste de Rochambeau, trapped and besieged a British army of 7,000, commanded by Charles Cornwallis. A British

fleet carrying reinforcements for Cornwallis reached Chesapeake Bay, but there was defeated by a French fleet. After that, Cornwallis surrendered. At that point the war had effectively ended. However, the final peace treaty was not signed until two years later, in 1783.

American soldiers endured a hard winter at Valley Forge, Pennsylvania, in late 1776 and early 1777, but survived to win the Revolution. These are modern "soldiers" wearing period uniforms at Valley Forge, today a historic park.

At Yorktown, Virginia, American and French forces won the decisive battle of the Revolution. The scene is recreated here by modern soldiers in the uniform of the time, with the British (in red) on the right.

Benjamin Franklin, shown here at his desk, was a key political figure in the developing American nation. He was also a noted printer, publisher, writer, scientist, and inventor.

The Confederation of the United States of America

The Treaty of Paris (1783) formally ended the American Revolution. Defeated Britain recognized American independence, and American territory stretched north to south from the Canadian border to the northern border of Florida; and west from the Atlantic to the Mississippi River. The lower Mississippi and West Florida (the Gulf Coast) went to Spain, under a separate British-Spanish treaty. Large portions of the northern, southern, and western borders of the United States were far from precisely settled by the peace treaty. These would be settled during the next half century, sometimes by negotiation and sometimes by war.

What still had to be fully established was the single nation that would be the United States of America. At the start of the Revolution, the rebelling British colonies had called themselves the United Colonies. The Continental Congress had been its wartime government. However, the individual colonial governments had continued to hold power in almost all colonial affairs.

In 1776 the Continental Congress had changed "United Colonies" to "United States." Then, while at war, the Congress set about forming an overall agreement among the colonies that would provide a common government. That agreement became the Articles of Confederation. It was introduced in 1777 and finally ratified on March 1, 1781, by Maryland, the last state to do so.

The Articles of Confederation established the Confederation of the United States of America, a loose alliance of the former British colonies. The Confederation government had very little independent power of its own. The 13 former colonies became the original 13 states of the Confederation. Each of these states had a largely independent government, with its own state constitution, government, and set of laws.

The national government of the Confederation consisted of a single House of Congress, in which each state had one vote. The delegates to Congress were selected by the state legislatures. The Congress could not raise money or regulate commerce without the unanimous agreement of all the states—and that was very seldom achieved. Nor was there any kind of real national government. Instead, the delegates to the Confederation Congress ran such government as there was with congressional committees.

In short, there was hardly any United States national government at all, and everything depended on the unanimous cooperation of the states. Yet in spite of that vacuum at the top, several important things happened in the new nation between the end of the Revolutionary War in 1783 and the creation of the Constitution in 1789 (see pp. 45–56).

The American ambassador to France, Benjamin Franklin (right) is shown here with a British representative negotiating the Treaty of Paris (1783), which formally ended the American Revolution.

The Frontier

The United States in 1783 was a big country, stretching from the Atlantic Ocean to the Mississippi River. However, most of the new country, from the Appalachian Mountains to the Mississippi, was held by Native Americans. That would change very quickly, for after the Revolution United States settlers began to pour west.

In the late 1780s the first wave of what would become millions of settlers began to move out of New England into central and western New York State on the Mohawk Trail. In the same period emigrants from the mid-Atlantic states began to pour west out of Philadelphia on the Pennsylvania Road, across Pennsylvania to Pittsburgh, and into the Ohio Valley. Through Cumberland Gap into Kentucky went tens of thousands more, on the Wilderness Road that Daniel Boone and his axemen had cleared. Farther south, settlers moved through the Appalachians to Nashville and out to the Mississippi on the Tennessee Path. (See Vol. 3, pp. 14–25, for more on all of these routes, including maps.)

South of the Appalachians, large numbers of American settlers moved west through Georgia. There they defeated and pushed back resisting Native-American forces, most of whom had allied themselves with Spain in response to American pressure. Despite the Spanish alliance, Native-American forces were eventually driven back everywhere, as a flood tide of American soldiers and settlers pushed west, taking and holding Native-American lands (see Vol. 2, p. 36, and Vol. 3, p. 34).

A Glimpse of Kentucky, from Cumberland Gap.

This early image shows a wagon passing through Cumberland Gap, a difficult but passable route through the Appalachian Mountains into Kentucky.

Many images from the early United States show conflict between settlers and Native Americans. In this one, The Hunter's Stratagem, the settlers are shown to be setting up an ambush by luring Native Americans into an attack with stuffed dummies.

Confederation Land Policy

The land policy of the Confederation had a great deal to do with the massive migration west that began after the American Revolution. That would continue to be so after adoption of the U.S. Constitution, for the new federal government continued the same policy.

The Land Ordinance of 1785 began to set the patterns that would be followed throughout the 1800s. It provided for surveys of government-owned lands, and for division of those lands into townships six miles square—that is, into townships each containing 36 square miles. Each township was then divided into sections of one square mile (640 acres) each, with one square mile set aside for schools. Sections were also further divided, down to quarter sections (40 acres), the smallest subdivision that could be bought.

The national government auctioned off township lands to private owners. Half of the townships were sold as whole 36-square-mile townships and half in one-square-mile sections.

The minimum price, originally set at one dollar per acre, was raised to two dollars in 1796. In the early years, land could be bought from the government only for cash. For a long period in later years, it could

Many roads westward followed Native-American foot trails. Wider paths were then carved out of the forests, like the rough trail being used by these men on horseback, in an image from the Crockett Almanac of the late 1830s.

also be bought on credit (see Vol. 3, pp. 55 and 72). Later, too, the minimum amount of land that could be bought at auction from the government was set at 80 acres, and the minimum price was reduced to $1.25 per acre.

As a practical matter, much of the land auctioned off by the government fell into the hands of speculators. They generally bought the land very cheaply and resold it at high profit to small farmers. Later much southern public land was also sold to large cotton planters. In some times and places, speculators bid land prices up too high for most small farmers.

Even so, most of the land still wound up in the hands of small farmers—and for them it was often good, cheap land that could be and was used to build family farms. The great flood of farm products they went on to produce built an inland empire.

The Northwest Ordinance

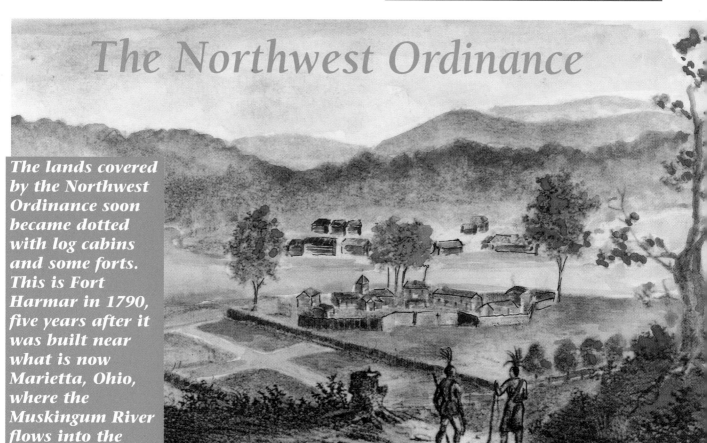

The lands covered by the Northwest Ordinance soon became dotted with log cabins and some forts. This is Fort Harmar in 1790, five years after it was built near what is now Marietta, Ohio, where the Muskingum River flows into the Ohio River.

The most substantial successes of the Confederation as a national government came on the frontier. In the Northwest Ordinance of 1787, the states of the Confederation managed to agree on ceding their huge western land claims to the nation. With the Land Ordinance of 1785 and the Northwest Ordinance of 1787 both in place, a mass of emigrants poured into the Northwest.

The Northwest Ordinance set the rules for admitting new states into the Union. Those rules have been followed throughout the United States, with some changes, for more than 200 years. For the original Northwest Territory, it provided that a total of three to five states could be carved out of the Territory. In the end, five new states would be formed from the Northwest Territory: Ohio, Indiana, Illinois, Michigan, and Wisconsin.

The Ordinance also banned slavery in all states created out of the Northwest Terri-

This small log cabin was the first house in Greene County, Ohio, built in 1798.

49

As American settlers began to move into Ohio, they were entering land long settled by Native Americans. The people of the Hopewell Culture, who lived in the area between 200 B.C. and 500 A.D., built great mounds, some of which survive today. At the right is a modern artist's view of a Hopewell religious leader performing a ceremony. Above are some earthworks that survive in "Mound City," in what is now part of the Hopewell Culture National Historic Park.

tory. That provision would have an enormous impact on the history of the United States.

The Ordinance provided two basic steps to statehood, each based on reaching a stated population level. At the start, an area was governed by Congress, which appointed a governor and three judges, who together would administer the area. After reaching a population of 5,000, that area could become a U.S. Territory. Then it would elect a state legislature, which would send a non-voting delegate to the national Congress. When a Territory reached a population of 60,000, it was eligible for full statehood, with the same rights as all the other states of the Union.

The Ordinance provided that Congress was to pass a separate "Enabling Act" granting admission to each state applying for statehood. The Enabling Act would include any special requirements for the state—as when Congress after the Civil War required the Confederate states to prohibit slavery before they could be readmitted to the Union.

The U.S. Congress passed a similar act covering the Southwest Territory in 1790. That Act allowed slavery in states created in the Southwest Territory, which consisted only of Tennessee.

The Confederation Economy

During its short existence the Confederation ran into substantial economic problems. Britain and the West Indies officially cut off most trade with the American states, while Spain officially cut off American foreign trade moving down the Mississippi River through New Orleans. Largely because of those economic problems, the Confederation period has often been described as the "critical period" during the shaping of the American nation.

Yet even though it ran into economic problems and still lacked an effective central government, the Confederation showed developing strength on the economic side. With the Revolution won, the old British colonial restrictions on foreign trade were gone. American manufacturing began its long growth toward world power. American agriculture, now beginning to grow beyond

51

the Appalachians, began to feed and clothe fast-growing populations, provide goods for homegrown factories, and find markets abroad for its products.

A striking example of what independence meant to American commerce was the opening of the China trade. During the colonial period Britain had banned American ships from China, reserving the China trade for its British East India Company. But with independence came trade with China.

On February 21, 1784, the American ship *Empress of China* sailed out of New York harbor bound for China, with a cargo mostly of ginseng (a medicinal plant), furs,

and clothing. The ship reached Whampoa, on China's Pearl River, on August 18, 1784, beginning what would become the great United States trade with China. In 1785 the *Empress of China* successfully returned to New York.

By 1789 scores of American ships were routinely and very profitably trading with China. American furs were greatly prized in China, so a substantial three-way trade began: New England ships carried American manufactured goods around Cape Horn to the Pacific Northwest. There they traded those goods for American furs. Then they sailed on to China, where they traded the furs for Chinese goods prized highly in the United States.

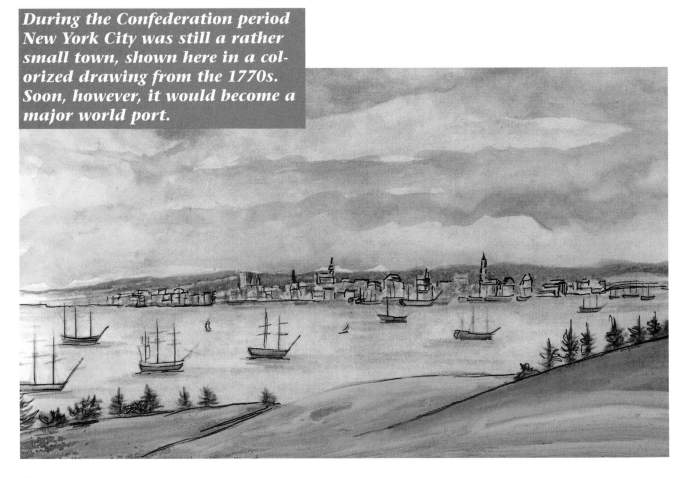

During the Confederation period New York City was still a rather small town, shown here in a colorized drawing from the 1770s. Soon, however, it would become a major world port.

In many parts of the new nation, the economy started small and grew slowly. This is the first hotel in Zanesville, Ohio, at what would become the intersection of Market and Second Streets in a prosperous and busy city.

British and Spanish restrictions against American trade also did not hold at all well. The British, Dutch, French, and Spanish colonies in the Caribbean all greatly needed American food, tobacco, lumber, and other products, as did the Netherlands, France, and Britain itself. As a result, American products quickly began to find their way into the Caribbean and across the Atlantic to Europe.

With independence also came freedom to build American finance and industry. American banks, investment companies, and manufacturers were organized soon after independence was won. By 1784 the Bank of New York, the Bank of North America, and the Massachusetts Bank of Boston had all been established. Investment companies were heavily financing the purchase of western lands for resale to farmers and planters. Cotton and woolen factories were being built in the New England and mid-Atlantic states, along with lumber mills, iron works, and stagecoach works.

The new nation was beginning to grow, though not without the problems created by sometimes too fast and too speculative growth. An economic depression came in 1784 and 1785, as many lenders tightened credit. They were responding to the failure of some land speculators and over-expansion in some industries. Another problem was damaging competition among the independent states of the Confederation.

During the summer of 1787 delegates to the Constitutional Convention in Philadelphia vigorously discussed questions of federation and confederation. Benjamin Franklin (center left, in brown) was a key figure in these discussions and unofficial host of the convention. Here he was talking with Alexander Hamilton (center right) and others, while taking some refreshment outdoors.

Confederation or Federation?

In the years following the Revolution, most Europeans and many Americans thought that the new Confederation had very little chance of surviving. Most expected that the states would quickly split apart into separate groups of small countries, which would then be gobbled up by the European powers in a continuation of their long conflict over North America.

At the same time, many American leaders felt that the only possible way to survive in a far-from-friendly world was to weld the states together into a single, expanding, united country. That became even more clear in 1786, when Massachusetts farmer Daniel Shays led thousands of farmers in a brief armed rebellion against state-ordered seizures of farms for unpaid taxes. The state militia was called out and put down the rebellion with very few casualties. The whole matter was later settled by a more sympathetic Massachusetts legislature, which pardoned Shays and his supporters.

Still, many Americans saw Shays' Rebellion as a very close call for the new nation. That incident built support for the formation of a new central government. Yet many people continued to have great fear of developing a repressive central government, for the experience of fighting soldiers of the British king was fresh in American memory.

Those who favored a strong new central government came to be called Federalists. Those who wanted to keep the Confederation government largely as it was became known as the Anti-Federalists. Leading Federalists included the first four Presidents of the United States: George Washington, John Adams, Thomas Jefferson, and James Madison. Washington had led the country through the Revolution. Adams had been a leading Revolutionary figure in Massachusetts. Jefferson had written the Declaration of Independence. Madison became a key figure in writing and pushing through the Constitution. Benjamin Franklin, long the new nation's elder statesman, was another leading Federalist.

There were highly respected figures on the Anti-Federalist side, too. Among them were leading Virginia Revolutionary leader Patrick Henry, future U.S. president James Monroe, and John Hancock, noted as the first signer of the Declaration of Independence.

There were also differences within the ranks of the Federalists. Many who wanted a strong federal govern-

Shays' Rebellion was an armed protest by farmers against the government seizing their land for unpaid taxes. It was one of the main challenges to the new state and national governments during the time of the Confederation of the United States.

ment were also deeply concerned that a new American brand of tyranny might grow that would destroy the freedoms they had just fought for and won. Some Federalists, along with many Anti-Federalists, feared that George Washington might become a new American king and sweep away democracy.

The largest—and in some ways the simplest—of all the questions facing Americans was that of "Confederation" or "Federation." The United States came out of the Revolution as a confederation—that is, as a group of 13 small independent nations, bound together by their shared history and their entirely voluntary agreement to act together for the common good. What the Federalists proposed—and won—was something entirely different. It was a federation that welded together those 13 small nations, converting them into 13 parts of a single nation, governed by a single national government.

That is the essence of what the Constitution did (see p. 57). Yet concerns ran deep about a strong central government, which could turn into a new tyranny. That led to the adoption of many compromises about which powers were to be held by the new central government and which kept by the states.

As they shaped their future, Americans were also concerned about how to safeguard the interests of smaller states, so that states with larger populations would not dominate the life of the new nation. Trying to deal with that problem led to a series of compromises on such matters as the nature of the houses of Congress and the rules governing national elections. Some of these problems would continue to generate raging controversy right on into the 21st century.

This is a picture of Philadelphia's Independence Hall in the period when revolutionaries declared their independence and later framed (designed) the Constitution of a new nation.

This is Howard Chandler Christy's painting **The Signing of the Constitution.** *The figure standing at the right is George Washington, who presided over the Constitutional Convention.*

The Constitution

On May 25, 1787, the Constitutional Convention opened at Philadelphia's Old State House, now known as Independence Hall. This is the most historic of all American buildings. It is where the Declaration of Independence was signed in 1776, the Articles of Confederation were adopted in 1781, and the Constitution was hammered out in 1787. Not all of the 55 delegates were present at the opening of the convention; many were still on the way.

Twelve of the original 13 states were represented; only Rhode Island did not send delegates, though it later ratified the

The Constitution of the United States was written and approved in this building, now called Independence Hall, in Philadelphia, Pennsylvania. It is also where the Declaration of Independence and the Articles of Confederation were signed.

new Constitution. Every state had only one vote at the convention, no matter how many delegates it had sent to Philadelphia.

George Washington, who had led the country from the start, was elected president of the convention. James Madison, who would become the chief architect of the Constitution, became unofficial secretary of the convention. Benjamin Franklin of Philadelphia was a delegate; America's elder statesman, then 81 years old, he was the unofficial host of the convention. Future presidents John Adams and Thomas Jefferson did not attend; they were both abroad on the nation's business.

All of the delegates were men, and all were White. There were no women or African-American or Native-American delegates.

The Constitutional Convention lasted almost four months,

through a long, hot Philadelphia summer. In those months the basic structures of the new American nation emerged, generally as compromises reached after long, exhausting, often-deadlocked sessions.

Many questions were not solved, but instead postponed, to be later settled by Congress, the courts, and, in the case of slavery, by the Civil War (see Vol. 5). Many of these questions still remain, and others have been added, into the 21st century, for the American system that began to be created by the Constitution was one that was able to develop and change.

On the greatest question facing them, the delegates agreed: They had originally been called together to make changes in the Articles of Confederation. Instead, they decided to completely scrap the Confederation, replacing it with a strong new national government—but one with safeguards against what they considered to be possible abuses of power.

In one of the most important compromises reached, the new government was to consist of two houses of Congress. The Senate would have two senators from each state, whatever its size, with both elected by the state legislatures. (Direct election of senators came only much later, in

In the days before typewriters, computers, and photocopiers, documents were written by hand, using quill pens and ink, as on this desk from Independence Hall, where the Declaration of Independence and the Constitution were both written. Once finished, these key documents would be set in type—also a hand process at the time—so printed copies could be sent around the country. However, the documents the delegates signed were written by hand.

1913.) The House of Representatives would be directly elected, with each member elected from a congressional district. The number of representatives depended on the size of a state's population.

Several key provisions favored the slave states—that is, those states that still had slavery. (Some states had already banned slavery.) The first, and most important, provision was the "three-fifths compromise." This provided that three-fifths of the slaves in a state would be counted for population purposes when setting the number of congressional representatives for each state. A second major compromise provided that the international slave trade could not be abolished until 1808. Another compromise provided that runaway slaves could not be protected by the free states—that is, states that had banned slavery.

One of the key aims of the Constitution was to set up three separate branches of government within a system of "checks and balances." The three branches were designed to be balanced against each other, so that no branch, individual, or group could create a runaway federal government, able to rule the country and destroy democracy.

The three branches were: the executive branch, led by the President; the Congress (the legislative branch), consisting of the Senate and House of Representatives; and the federal courts (the judicial branch), with final authority resting in the Supreme Court. At the start, the power of the Supreme Court as the final interpreter of the nation's laws was not written into the Constitution. However, that power was soon taken by the Court and accepted as a basic part of the American system (see Vol. 2, p. 53).

Beyond federal checks and balances, the Constitution reserved many important powers for the states, rather than making the new central government all-powerful. Among these was the power to accept, alter, or reject proposed amendments of the Constitution itself. Some key powers were solely federal powers, including the ability to make war, conduct foreign affairs, regulate foreign and interstate trade, and coin money. However, most other powers were to be reserved to the states.

One example of how the "checks and balances" system worked was in the election of the President, head of the new exec-

President of the Constitutional Convention, George Washington (center) had earlier been Commander-in-Chief of the Continental Army and would later be the first President of the United States.

utive branch. The Constitution provided that the President was to be elected by the Electoral College. This was composed of groups of state electors, selected under rules set separately by each state legislature. The numbers of electors for each state was decided by that state's number of Congressional Representatives. At the start, the state legislatures had various ways of choosing electors, but soon electors were directly elected by the legislature in almost all states. By the late 1820s most states had decided to choose electors by popular vote. Today all electors are selected by popular vote.

Once elected, the President was far from all-powerful. The President's Cabinet and Supreme Court nominees, as well as large numbers of other presidential nominations, were subject to approval by the Senate. The President could veto (refuse to sign) new laws passed by Congress. However, two-thirds of the Senate and House of Representatives could override that veto and so enact the law over the presidential veto. The President could call for a declaration of war, but needed congressional approval of it. The President could negotiate and propose treaties, but the Senate had to ratify (formally approve) those treaties. The President could also be impeached and removed from office by Congress, if the House indicted and the Senate voted to remove the President from office.

The Congress also could not become all-powerful, for a series of brakes on its power were written into the Constitution. The Supreme Court could undo a law by ruling it unconstitutional. Then an amendment to the Constitution would be needed to make that law enforceable. Above all, the Constitution was established as "the Supreme Law of the land," as were those laws and treaties made under its authority. It was to be interpreted as that supreme law by all United States federal and state judges.

> *The basis of our government being the opinion of the people, the very first object should be to keep that right; and were it left to me to decide whether we should have a government without newspapers, or newspapers without a government, I should not hesitate a moment to prefer the latter.*
>
> THOMAS JEFFERSON, IN A LETTER ON JANUARY 16, 1787.

Finally, it was impossible under the terms of the Constitution for the third branch of government, the federal courts, to become all-powerful. Though the Supreme Court became the final interpreter of the Constitution, it had no executive or legislative powers. Therefore it could not propose, pass, or enforce any laws. It could not in any way govern; it interpreted.

The Constitutional Convention ended on September 17, 1787, with 39 of the 55 delegates signing the completed document. (For the full text of the original Constitution, see Vol. 10, p. 69.)

The final approval of the U.S. Constitution—and therefore the official founding of the United States—was greeted with great celebration around the country. On Wall Street in New York City, the 1788 celebration included this float of the "Ship of State."

Adopting the Constitution

The Constitution's final hurdle lay ahead, for it still had be ratified (formally approved) by the states. That meant a long, very difficult campaign that might very well have resulted in failure. Most Americans shared tremendous mistrust of central government, and Anti-Federalist forces were still strong throughout the country.

The Constitution required that nine of the original 13 states ratify it before it could become the ruling law of the United States. When a state ratified the Constitution, it became an original state of the new federal Union (see p. 84). As a practical matter, however, it was clear that—no matter how many small states accepted the Constitution—ratification by the big states of Pennsylvania, Massachusetts, Virginia, and New York would be necessary for the formation of the new nation.

Despite Anti-Federalist opposition, the first five states to ratify did so quickly and easily. Delaware was the first (December 7, 1787), followed by Pennsylvania, New Jersey, Georgia, and Connecticut. Massachusetts came next, in a close vote, followed by Maryland, South Carolina, and New Hampshire, which was the ninth state to ratify the Constitution, on June 21, 1788.

Although New Hampshire's ratification legally created the Union and made the Constitution the law of the new nation, it took very close votes in Virginia and New York to complete working acceptance of the Constitution by the states. North Carolina and Rhode Island ratified later, becoming the twelfth and thirteenth states of the Union.

A great and very direct goal for an overwhelming majority of Americans was the establishment of a set of American birthrights, the "unalienable rights" that were at the heart of the Declaration of Independence (see p. 38). Those birthrights had to be put plainly, and it had to be made perfectly clear that no one could take them away. That goal would be met by the first ten Amendments to the Constitution—that is, the Bill of Rights (see p. 70). Other Amendments would be added in later times. Some other key questions were left unresolved (see pp. 77–78).

The framers (designers) of the original Constitution focused on creating a new, workable government, building in many centrally important checks and balances to protect Americans against a possible new tyranny. During that process they had postponed a clear statement of the personal and political freedoms guaranteed to all Americans. It was expected by all, though. Indeed, the Constitution would probably have been defeated if its framers had not promised a Bill of Rights as their first order of business after forming the new government. That was made very clear during the course of ratification, as state after state convention passed Bills of Rights demands as a condition for ratifying the Constitution.

In the days before radio, television, telephones, telegraphs, cars, and railroads, information traveled slowly. People and newspapers would often travel by coaches like this Elizabeth Town stage-wagon to Philadelphia, advertised in a 1781 newspaper.

The First National Government

George Washington (center) was sworn in as the first President of the United States on April 30, 1789, at Federal Hall in New York City.

And so it began. The United States of America was no longer a collection of 13 independent nations. Now it had become a single new nation.

The next step was to create a national government. The process of electing the first Congress under the Constitution began in the autumn of 1788 and was completed during the spring of 1789. Federalists dominated both the Senate and the House of Representatives in this first United States Congress, which swiftly moved to develop a fully national government.

George Washington—who had led the country through the Revolution, the Confederation, and the adoption of the Constitution—became the first President of the new United States. On January 17, 1789, he was unanimously elected to the Presidency by the members of the new Electoral College.

In this first presidential election each

elector voted for two candidates. Washington was the unanimous first-vote choice. The delegates' second votes were split up among eleven other candidates. Altogether Washington received 69 electoral votes. John Adams, who came in second with 34 electoral votes, became the country's first Vice President.

The first capital of the United States was New York City. There, at Federal Hall, the first Congress was formally called to order on April 6, 1789, to begin the business of creating a new American government.

> *Our Constitution is in actual operation; everything appears to promise that it will last; but in this world nothing is certain but death and taxes.*
>
> BENJAMIN FRANKLIN, IN A LETTER TO M. LEROY, 1789.

There, on April 30, 1789, George Washington was inaugurated as first President of the United States.

Washington then proceeded to form the first executive branch of the new government. For his Secretary of State, he chose Thomas Jefferson of Virginia, author of the Declaration of Independence, ambassador to France during the Revolution, and a future two-term President of the United States. As Secretary of the Treasury, he chose Alexander Hamilton of New York, who would become the chief architect of the federal financial system. His Secretary of War was Revolutionary War general Henry Knox. The first Attorney General of the United States was former Virginia governor Edmund Randolph.

The members of the first Cabinet, the President's key advisors, are shown here: (from left) Henry Knox, Secretary of War; Thomas Jefferson, Secretary of State; Edmund Randolph, Attorney General; and Alexander Hamilton, Secretary of the Treasury.

The third branch of the United States government is the federal court system. The Constitution dealt with the power of the Supreme Court to interpret the laws and actions of the other branches of government. It also set up the general outlines of the new federal court system. However, it remained for the first Congress to create that court system. It did that in the Judiciary Act of 1789. This provided for 13 lowest-level federal district courts; three second-level circuit courts, which handled appeals from the district courts; and at its top a six-member Supreme Court.

Like Congress and the Presidency, the federal court system created in 1789 still exists and works, though with some changes over the centuries. Defining the full power of the Supreme Court, however, was not accomplished by either the Constitution or the Judiciary Act. That took much longer.

Congress set up the federal court system. Then it was up to the President to appoint its judges with the consent of Congress, as its still true today. President Washington appointed John Jay of New York as the first Chief Justice of the U.S. Supreme Court. Jay had been a leading diplomat during the Revolution, Secretary for Foreign Affairs of the Confederation, and the first Chief Justice of the New York State court system.

The Congress of the United States first met at Federal Hall on Wall Street in New York City, then the nation's capital, on April 6, 1789. That building no longer exists, but this new Federal Hall serves as a museum of that time.

George Washington

This is a young George Washington, painted in his Virginia militia uniform by John Gadsby Chapman.

Revolutionary War Commander-in-Chief, President of the Constitutional Convention, first President of the United States—George Washington (1732–1799) was by any measure the leading American public figure of his time.

Washington started his working life in 1749, as a surveyor in Culpeper County, Virginia. He inherited his plantation at Mount Vernon, Virginia, in 1752; it was his lifelong home. He began the first phase of his military career in 1753 as a young officer in the Virginia militia. In 1754 he became a lieutenant-colonel and later colonel in the Virginia militia. He built and was forced to surrender Fort Necessity, near modern Pittsburgh, Pennsylvania, to the French in 1754. He also led the Virginia militia during British general Braddock's major defeat in 1755.

Washington was commander of the Virginia militia until the end of the French and Indian War in 1763. He then retired to private life, but he soon entered political life as a delegate to the Virginia House of

Burgesses. During the run-up to the American Revolution, he was a firm supporter of the American side, favoring armed resistance.

In 1775 Washington became Commander-in-Chief of the Continental Army. He then led his forces and the new American nation through eight years of war. The American army in 1775 was a raw militia. However, with his leadership, and often suffering defeat after defeat, it became the seasoned force that survived the winter of 1777–1778 at Valley Forge and went on to capture Cornwallis's army at Yorktown in 1781 (see p. 40), effectively ending the war.

After the war, during the Confederation period, Washington was a prime mover in pulling the nearly independent states of the Confederation into the federal Union. He served as President of the Constitutional Convention, and then became the first President of the United States (1789–1796). In office,

and against tremendous odds, he took the lead in organizing the new nation and holding it together, much to the surprise of the European powers of the day, while avoiding war with either France or Britain—an even more remarkable accomplishment.

In his private life Washington was a large-scale Virginia planter of his time. Like many other Southerners, including Thomas Jefferson, he held slaves and owned plantations that prospered by using the labor of those slaves. And like many other well-to-do Americans of his time, he also speculated in western lands.

George Washington died at Mount Vernon, Virginia, on December 10, 1799.

George Washington arrived for his 1789 presidential inauguration in New York City by boat, to great celebration.

This is an early U.S. Supreme Court in historic Independence Hall in Philadelphia, Pennsylvania.

The Bill of Rights

One of the greatest accomplishments of the new Congress—and of the new American nation—was passage of the Bill of Rights. These rights were set forth in the first ten Amendments to the Constitution. Written mainly by future president James Madison, the Bill of Rights Amendments were enacted by Congress on September 25, 1789, and then sent to the states for ratification. Three quarters of the states had to ratify the Bill of Rights for these Amendments to become part of the Constitution. That process was completed on December 15, 1791, when Virginia became the tenth state to ratify the Bill of Rights.

The provisions of the Bill of Rights are not the only parts of the Constitution that deal with the rights of Americans. The seven original sections of the Constitution guarantee some other key rights (see p. 76). Yet without the Bill of Rights the original Constitution was unfinished, for the Bill of Rights covered much of what the new American democracy was all about, from long before there was a new American nation.

70

Ratification of the Bill of Rights completed the bedrock of the Constitution. But to describe these as "bedrock" is not to imply that, once written, the Constitution was "set in stone," never to be changed. Far from it; the Constitution was and is a living document that has grown and changed a great deal during the more than two centuries of the American republic.

Over those centuries new Amendments and Supreme Court rulings have gone far to extend the freedoms guaranteed by the Constitution to many who were left out or shortchanged earlier (see p. 78). Among them were African Americans, Native Americans, women, Asian Americans, and many other religious, ethnic, and social groups. A great many Americans carefully

As the first Chief Justice of the U.S. Supreme Court, John Jay was also the first to interpret and enforce the Bill of Rights added to the Constitution.

watch and protect their freedoms. That has always meant, first of all, watching and protecting the Constitution and the Bill of Rights.

Bills of rights became part of American life soon after the British colonies were established. One of the earliest was the Massachusetts Body of Liberties (1641). This established many of the rights that would be made part of the Constitution 150 years later. Another was the Charter of Rhode Island (1644). That charter established a great deal of religious freedom in Rhode Island from the beginning. A third was Pennsylvania's Frame of Government (1682). That document established a large measure of religious freedom and the right to trial by jury in criminal cases.

Virginia became the first state to adopt a Bill of Rights as part of its new state constitution in 1776. By 1777, 11 more states had constitutions, and seven of these included bills of rights. The first bill of rights passed by the national government was included in the Northwest Ordinance (1787), which also outlawed slavery in the Northwest Territory.

Following is the Bill of Rights, the first ten Amendments (sometimes called Articles) to the Constitution. Note that although they are briefly stated, every one of the freedoms they guarantee has been the basis of a huge body of law, and each has been tested and modified by many Supreme Court decisions. Yet note also—and very carefully— that every one of the freedoms guaranteed by the Bill of Rights is alive today and belongs to every American.

The First Amendment guarantees:

- ★ Freedom of religion.
- ★ Freedom of speech.
- ★ Freedom of the press.
- ★ Freedom to gather peacefully.
- ★ Freedom to call upon the government to set right people's grievances.

Amendment I

Congress shall make no law respecting an establishment of religion, or prohibiting the free exercise thereof; or abridging the freedom of speech, or of the press; or the right of the people peaceably to assemble, and to petition the Government for a redress of grievances.

The Second Amendment guarantees:

- ★ The right to keep and bear arms. (What that means as a practical matter is now, as much as ever before, a matter of often-heated public debate.)

Amendment II

A well regulated Militia, being necessary to the security of a free State, the right of the people to keep and bear Arms, shall not be infringed.

The Third Amendment guarantees:

- ★ That in peacetime no home can be used to house soldiers without the consent of the homeowner.
- ★ That in wartime no home can be used to house soldiers except as allowed by law. On the eve of the American Revolution, the British Coercive Acts had forced Americans to quarter British troops in their homes, and that abuse of citizens was banned by the Third Amendment.

Amendment III

No soldier shall, in time of peace be quartered in any house, without the consent of the Owner, nor in time of war, but in a manner to be prescribed by law.

The Fourth Amendment guarantees:
- ★ The people's right to be protected against "unreasonable searches and seizures" by the government of themselves, and of their houses, papers, and other property. What is "unreasonable" has often had to be decided by the courts.
- ★ That any warrants authorizing searches and seizures be issued only if there is thought to be "probable cause," as supported by sworn or other legally acceptable statements; and that the warrant must clearly state what place is to be searched, and what may be seized.

Amendment IV

The right of the people to be secure in their persons, houses, papers, and effects, against unreasonable searches and seizures, shall not be violated, and no Warrants shall issue, but upon probable cause, supported by Oath or affirmation, and particularly describing the place to be searched, and the persons or things to be seized.

The Fifth Amendment guarantees:
- ★ That a grand jury must authorize charges in all criminal cases involving a possible death penalty, except charges against a member of the armed forces in wartime or other "public danger."
- ★ That no one can be tried twice for the same alleged crime. This is the protection against "double jeopardy."
- ★ That no one charged with a crime can be forced to testify against himself or herself. This is the protection against "self-incrimination."
- ★ That all are entitled to "due process of law" before being "deprived of life, liberty, or property."
- ★ That government cannot take private property without paying a fair price to its owners.

Amendment V

No person shall be held to answer for a capital, or otherwise infamous crime, unless on a presentment or indictment of a Grand Jury, except in cases arising in the land or naval forces, or in the Militia, when in actual service in time of War or public danger; nor shall any person be subject for the same offence to be twice put in jeopardy of life or limb; nor shall be compelled in any criminal case to be a witness against himself, nor be deprived of life, liberty, or property, without due process of law; nor shall private property be taken for public use, without just compensation.

The Sixth Amendment guarantees:

That all defendants in criminal cases have:

★ The right to a quick and public trial.

★ The right to be tried by an impartial jury, and in the state and district where the alleged crime was committed.

★ The right to be informed of the charges against them, and of the causes of those charges.

★ The right to directly face the witnesses against them, and to legally require the testimony of favorable witnesses.

★ The right to have lawyers or other counsel to defend them.

Trial by jury in criminal cases is also provided by Article III, Section 2 of the Constitution, but Amendment VI of the Bill of Rights adds several safeguards for the defendant.

Amendment VI

In all criminal prosecutions, the accused shall enjoy the right to a speedy and public trial, by an impartial jury of the State and district wherein the crime shall have been committed, which district shall have been previously ascertained by law, and to be informed of the nature and cause of the accusation; to be confronted with the witnesses against him; to have compulsory process for obtaining witnesses in his favor, and to have the Assistance of Counsel for his defence.

The Seventh Amendment guarantees:

★ The right to trial by jury in many noncriminal cases based on the "common law." Note that the "common law" is the main body of English law. This is nonwritten law, developed on the basis of rulings in similar cases that, in many instances, go back hundreds of years in Britain and the United States.

Amendment VII

In Suits at common law, where the value in controversy shall exceed twenty dollars, the right of trial by jury shall be preserved, and no fact tried by a jury, shall be otherwise re-examined in any Court of the United States, than according to the rules of the common law.

The Eighth Amendment guarantees:
- ★ That "excessive bail" not be required to free someone accused of a crime.
- ★ That "excessive fines" not be ordered by judges on those convicted of crimes.
- ★ That "cruel and unusual punishments" not be ordered by judges or inflicted by anyone on those convicted of crimes.

  Note that the ban on "cruel and unusual punishments" was a bar to the many kinds of tortures that were still then being practiced in many European countries—and that are still practiced in many parts of the world today.

Amendment VIII

Excessive bail shall not be required, nor excessive fines imposed, nor cruel and unusual punishments inflicted.

The Ninth Amendment guarantees:
- ★ That rights not named in the Constitution are in no way inferior to those in the Constitution, and that such rights are still held by the people.

Amendment IX

The enumeration in the Constitution, of certain rights, shall not be construed to deny or disparage others retained by the people.

The Tenth Amendment guarantees:
- ★ That the states, or the people, keep all rights not given by the states to the federal government, or barred to the states by the Constitution.

Amendment X

The powers not delegated to the United States by the Constitution, nor prohibited by it to the States, are reserved to the States respectively, or to the people.

Other Freedoms

The Liberty Bell in Philadelphia, Pennsylvania, got its name because it was rung to signal key events in American history, such as the first reading of the Declaration of Independence.

Several other freedoms were made part of the original Constitution. Among them are:

★ That a prisoner has the right to get a "writ of habeas corpus," which protects against being held unlawfully. This order, issued by a judge or court, forces law enforcement officers to produce a prisoner before a court or judge who may release the prisoner. (Article I, Section 9 of the Constitution.)

★ That no legislature, including Congress, can enact a "bill of attainder." This is a law that names a person guilty of a crime, usually treason, without a trial, and orders that the person named be executed. (Article I, Section 9 of the Constitution.)

★ That no legislature, including Congress, has the power to enact an "ex post facto" law. This is a law that is retroactive (applies to something that happened before the law existed). For example, an act cannot by law make something a crime that was not a crime when the act was being done. (Article I, Section 9 of the Constitution.)

★ That treason against the United States is limited only to making war against the United States, cooperating with its enemies, or giving aid and comfort to its enemies. (Article III, Section 3 of the Constitution.)

★ That although Congress has the power to set the punishment for treason, no conviction of treason can be punished beyond the life of the person convicted. This means that the family of someone convicted of treason cannot be punished by loss of their rights as Americans or by forfeiture (loss) of their property. (Article III, Section 3 of the Constitution.)

The Question of Secession

Some other major questions and disagreements were not solved at all by the Constitution. One was the question of the "right" to secede (withdraw) from the Union, even if that meant dissolving the United States of America.

This "right" to secede was insisted on during western Pennsylvania's Whiskey Rebellion in 1794 (see Vol. 2, p. 13). Far more seriously, it was insisted on by many in the South three times between the adoption of the Constitution and the Civil War. Each time this generated a crisis that threatened to destroy the Union.

In 1820 secession was threatened on the issue of whether or not new states admitted into the Union would be slave or free (see Vol. 3, p. 58). The South withdrew its threat to secede after the Missouri Compromise postponed the question of slavery once again.

In the early 1830s, the South again threatened to secede, this time on tax issues. It withdrew its threat only when President Andrew Jackson prepared to use force to stop secession, if necessary (see Vol. 3, p. 67).

In 1860 the threat of secession was directly intertwined with by far the deepest of all American issues: the abolition or continuance of slavery. This time the issue was not resolved peacefully. All together, the issues of slavery, secession, and the preservation of the Union tore the United States apart in the Civil War (see Vol. 5).

The idea of secession was very much alive on the frontier. People who had left their settled ways behind to move into new country often had little sympathy with a strong central government.

Slaves were among those not protected by the Constitution and the Bill of Rights when they were originally passed. The institution of slavery continued, and slaves often had to "bow and scrape" before plantation owners, as here, if they were to avoid punishment.

Unfinished Business

It is worth noting here that neither the Declaration of Independence nor the Constitution took steps to abolish slavery, or granted equal citizenship to Native Americans, or established equal rights for women. That would all come much later.

During the Revolutionary War far more African Americans fought on the British side than the American side, for the British freed any African American who fought with them. An estimated 35,000–40,000 African Americans did just that. Most of them fled from the new United States with the retreating British at war's end. Only an estimated 5,000–7,000 African Americans fought on the American side.

Far more Native Americans also fought on the British side. Among them were the Mohawks, who fled to Canada after the war. The then-depopulated Mohawk Valley became a major area of settlement and a great road west for millions of American settlers (see Vol. 3, p. 15).

The United States in 1790

$\mathcal{L}$ooking at it in one way, the new United States was a great, big, fast-growing country, with limitless possibilities. It had just won a war of independence against the world's greatest imperial power. Its people were pouring west to settle huge new tracts of land all the way to the Mississippi. Its economy was bouncing back after a deep depression during the Confederation period.

The first United States census was conducted in 1790, as directed by the Constitution. That called for a census within three years after the first meeting of the Congress, and then every ten years, as is still so today.

That first census counted a big country, of 865,000 square miles. In territory, the United States was far larger than Britain, France, and Spain together. Yet the new United States was still a quite small country in population. Britain, France, Spain, and

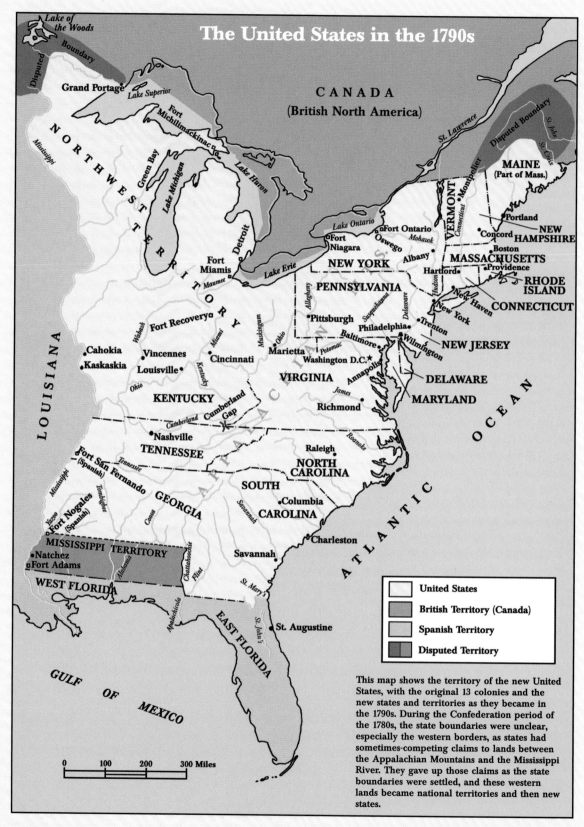

The United States in the 1790s

CANADA
(British North America)

Lake of the Woods

Disputed Boundary

Grand Portage

Lake Superior

Fort Michilimackinac

Disputed Boundary

St. Lawrence

St. John

St. Croix

MAINE
(Part of Mass.)

NORTHWEST TERRITORY

Mississippi

Green Bay

Lake Michigan

Lake Huron

Detroit

Fort Miamis

Maumee

Lake Erie

Lake Ontario

Fort Ontario

Fort Oswego

Fort Niagara

Mohawk

Albany

Montpelier

VERMONT

Connecticut

Portland

Concord

NEW HAMPSHIRE

Boston

MASSACHUSETTS

Providence

Hartford

RHODE ISLAND

NEW YORK

New Haven

CONNECTICUT

PENNSYLVANIA

Allegheny

Susquehanna

Delaware

Hudson

New York

Pittsburgh

Philadelphia

Trenton

NEW JERSEY

Fort Recovery

Wabash

Miami

Muskingum

Ohio

Baltimore

Wilmington

Fort Recovery

Cahokia

Kaskaskia

Vincennes

Louisville

Cincinnati

Marietta

Potomac

Washington D.C.★

Annapolis

DELAWARE

VIRGINIA

James

MARYLAND

Kentucky

Ohio

KENTUCKY

Cumberland

Cumberland Gap

Richmond

Roanoke

Nashville

TENNESSEE

Tennessee

Raleigh

NORTH CAROLINA

Fort San Fernando (Spanish)

Mississippi

GEORGIA

SOUTH CAROLINA

Columbia

Coosa

Tombigbee

Savannah

Charleston

Yazoo

Fort Nogales (Spanish)

MISSISSIPPI TERRITORY

Natchez

Fort Adams

Alabama

Chattahoochee

Flint

Savannah

St. Mary's

WEST FLORIDA

Apalachicola

EAST FLORIDA

St. John's

St. Augustine

LOUISIANA

APPALACHIAN

ATLANTIC OCEAN

GULF OF MEXICO

0   100   200   300 Miles

Legend

☐ United States
▨ British Territory (Canada)
▨ Spanish Territory
▨ Disputed Territory

This map shows the territory of the new United States, with the original 13 colonies and the new states and territories as they became in the 1790s. During the Confederation period of the 1780s, the state boundaries were unclear, especially the western borders, as states had sometimes-competing claims to lands between the Appalachian Mountains and the Mississippi River. They gave up those claims as the state boundaries were settled, and these western lands became national territories and then new states.

Estimated Percentage of Various Ethnic Backgrounds in the United States in 1790

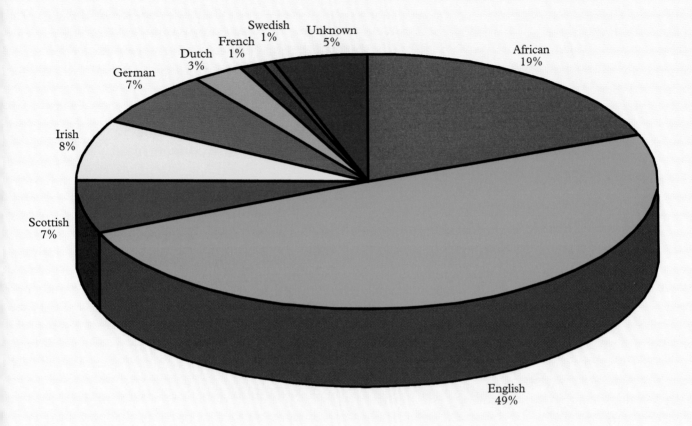

Russia—all rivals for North America—had far greater populations and military strength at this time.

The 1790 census indicated that the population of the United States was increasing at a great rate. From 2,780,000 in 1780, the U.S. population had grown to 3,929,000 in 1790, an increase of more than 41 percent. That population included 3,172,000 Whites (81 percent) and 757,000 African Americans (19 percent). There were probably 100,000 to 200,000 Native Americans in the United States; they were not included in the census figures.

Almost all of the White Americans had European roots. The English and Welsh formed the majority—56 percent—of the White population and 49 percent of the total U.S. population. (In the census the Welsh were counted in with the English.) People with Irish roots formed approximately 10 percent of the U.S. White population (8 percent of the total population). People from Germany and Scotland were each 8 percent of the U.S. White population (7 percent of the total).

Substantial numbers of Americans had Dutch, French, Swedish, and many other ethnic origins. The majorities in most of the colonies were of English or Welsh stock. Pennsylvania had large numbers of German Americans (35 percent), while New Jersey and New York had substantial numbers of Dutch, Irish, and Scottish Americans. There was no attempt made at that time to trace the national origins of either free or enslaved African Americans.

Most African Americans were slaves, though approximately 60,000 were free. The great majority of slaves were concentrated in Virginia, North Carolina, South Carolina, and Maryland.

At its start, the nation was in the early stages of a campaign to abolish slavery that would lead to the Civil War (see Vol. 5). Rhode Island had ended slavery in 1774 and Vermont in 1777. In 1780 Pennsylvania had become the first Confederation state to abolish slavery. In 1783 the Massachusetts courts had ruled that slavery in that state had been ended by the state constitution of 1780. New Hampshire had also ended slavery in 1783, as did Connecticut in 1784. New York in 1799 and New Jersey in 1804 would pass gradual emancipation (freedom) laws. The other six of the original 13 states—Delaware, Georgia, Maryland, North Carolina, South Carolina, and Virginia— remained slave states.

In the 1790s American roads were made of dirt, winding through forests and fields. This picture of a stagecoach leaving a roadside tavern is from Isaac Weld's 1798 book Travels Through the States of North America.

In 1790 and for decades more to come, houses were built of hand-cut beams of wood, fitted together with great skill and labor, as in this scene. Only decades later would houses be built with wood cut to standard sizes.

In 1790 more than 90 percent of Americans lived on farms or in small rural villages and towns, with very few living in cities. The most heavily populated section of the country was a strip running along the northeastern coast. This included the three largest cities—Philadelphia, New York, and Boston—but none had reached 50,000 in population.

As in colonial times, the roads were generally poor. That situation was worsened by eight years of war, followed by the years of state rule during the Confederation period.

Most Americans remained largely self-sufficient farmers. That would change as commerce and industry developed and as the cities grew. In 1790, however, roads had to be built, waterways needed to be widened and joined, and canals had to be created. Millions of people would move west on those roads and waterways, and later on what would become a continent-wide railroad network.

The Original 13

1787

Delaware *was the first state to be admitted to the Union, on December 7, 1787, as the first to ratify the Constitution (see p. 63). Earlier held by Sweden, it had been taken by Britain in 1644. Delaware was part of Pennsylvania until 1775, then treated as a separate state by the Continental Congress.*

Pennsylvania *was the second state to be admitted to the Union, on December 12, 1787. Its ownership had earlier been disputed by Britain, the Netherlands, and Sweden, but Pennsylvania was fully taken by Britain in 1664. It went to William Penn as a royal grant in 1681.*

New Jersey *was the third state to be admitted to the Union, on December 18, 1787. Originally settled by the Dutch, it was taken by Britain in 1664. New Jersey was part of New York until 1775, then sending its own delegates to the Continental Congress.*

1788

Georgia *was the fourth state to be admitted to the Union, on January 2, 1788. Settled by the British in 1733, it grew slowly during colonial times. Georgia was the first southern state to ratify the Constitution.*

Connecticut *was the fifth state to be admitted to the Union, on January 9, 1788. Originally part of Massachusetts, the Connecticut Colony was founded in the late 1630s, and the New Haven Colony in 1643. Both were joined as the Connecticut Colony in 1662.*

Massachusetts *was the sixth state to be admitted to the Union, on February 6, 1788. First settled by the Pilgrims in 1620, and later the most important of the New England colonies, Massachusetts played a major role in the American Revolution.*

Maryland *was the seventh state to be admitted to the Union, on April 28, 1788. Earlier part of Virginia, Maryland had become a royal colony in 1632 and was settled in the same year.*

States of the Union

1788

South Carolina was the eighth state to be admitted to the Union, on May 23, 1788. Originally claimed by France, Spain, and Britain, it had received its royal charter as a British crown colony in 1663.

New Hampshire was the ninth state to be admitted to the Union, on June 21, 1788. First settled in 1623, it had been part of Massachusetts until becoming a royal colony in 1679. With New Hampshire's ratification, the Union was formally created (see p. 63).

Virginia was the tenth state to be admitted to the Union, on June 25, 1788. Founded in 1607, Virginia's Jamestown settlement had been the first successful British colony on the North American mainland. Virginia went on to become the center of British settlement in the South.

1788

New York was the eleventh state to be admitted to the Union, on July 26, 1788. It had been settled in 1625, originally as the Dutch New Netherlands colony. It was taken by Britain in 1644.

1789

North Carolina was the twelfth state to be admitted to the Union, on November 21, 1789. The site of two early, failed British settlements in the 1580s, it had been settled successfully in the 1650s, becoming a royal crown colony in 1663.

1790

Rhode Island was the thirteenth state to be admitted to the Union, on May 29, 1790. Settled by the British in the 1630s, Rhode Island was founded by religious freedom advocate Roger Williams in 1638 and was chartered as a colony by Britain's Parliament in 1644.

(For more information on the growth of the states, see Vol. 10, p. 62.)

In the late 1700s and early 1800s, Spain held California with a string of fortified missions. One of them was Carmel Mission, today preserved as a historic site.

Facing the World

Despite all its growth and promise, the United States was in 1790 still a very small, weak country, facing a world full of much stronger powers. Its population was largely agricultural, and its budding industries were small. Although it faced several of the world's greatest military and imperial pow-

ers, it had a very small, ill-equipped army, hardly any navy at all, little money with which to buy arms, and a tiny homegrown armaments industry. Britain, a great power, had four times the U.S. population and the world's greatest navy. It was also in the process of building a worldwide empire, which included Canada. The British still held seven forts in the Old Northwest and were allied with Native-American nations in that area. Many in Britain wanted to get back at least a substantial part of the United States.

France, also a great power, had more than four times the American population and powerful military forces. The French Revolution, in 1789, was the trigger that started a whole new series of European wars, with revolutionary France confronting most of the other European great powers (see Vol. 2, p. 22). Within a few years Napoleon Bonaparte would take power in France and conquer most of Europe. A massive new world war was developing, just as the small, fragile new American nation was beginning to spread its wings. Many in France had never fully accepted the loss of North America to the British. And many Americans now saw Republican France as a new and major enemy.

Spain, which had fought against American forces during the American Revolution, held Florida, the Gulf Coast, the lower Mississippi River, the Southwest, and California. Its huge empire also included all of South and Central America, except for Brazil.

Spain was also allied with and supplied arms to the Native-American nations of the Southeast, including the Cherokees and Creeks. By the late 1700s, Spain had also established a string of fortified Catholic missions on the California coast, as far north as San Francisco, along a route called El Camino Real (The Royal Road). Yet Spain was a weakening great power and was beginning to lose its empire in the Americas. Soon there would be successful colonial revolutions in many countries, all the way from Mexico to the tip of South America (see Vol. 3, p. 9).

The powerful Russian Empire, which had been expanding eastward across Eurasia for three centuries, had also established itself in North America. By the late 1700s, Russian traders, trappers, and soldiers were operating from bases in Alaska. Russian ships were competing with the Americans and British for Pacific sea otters and in the very profitable China trade. The Russians clearly planned to colonize the American West Coast. They did, in fact, move south into northern California in the early 1800s (see Vol. 3, p. 11).

For the new United States, in 1790, everything seemed possible—and most of what seemed possible did happen, ultimately turning the country into a massive world power. In 1790, though, almost all of it still remained to be done.

The British and their Native-American allies remained just across the northern border in Canada, a potential threat to the new United States. Many lived in wooden forts like this reconstructed village in what is now the province of Ontario.

On the Internet

The Internet has many interesting and useful sites. However, the site addresses often change. The best way to find current addresses is to go to a search site, such as **www.yahoo.com**. As this book was being written, websites relating to this volume included:

http://www.nara.gov/exhall/charters/constitution/conmain.html
The Constitution of the United States, a site from the National Archives and Records Administration (NARA), including images and text of the original documents, biographies of the signers, and articles about the Constitutional Convention and the ratification process. Student activities and lesson plans are offered at:
http://www.nara.gov/education/teaching/constitution/home.html
Similar information on the Declaration of Independence is at:
http://www.nara.gov/exhall/charters/declaration/decmain.html

http://www.access.gpo.gov/congress/senate/constitution/toc.html
The Constitution of the United States of America, a site of the Congressional Research Service of the Library of Congress, a searchable database including historical information on the Constitution and key Supreme Court decisions.

http://www.fordham.edu/halsall/mod/modsbook07.html
http://www.fordham.edu/halsall/mod/modsbook12.html
Sections of the Internet Modern History Sourcebook, offering links to many documents on Colonial North America, the fight for American independence, and the establishment of the United States, including materials on Native Americans and slavery.

http://www.ukans.edu/history/VL/USA/ERAS/discovery.html
http://www.ukans.edu/history/VL/USA/ERAS/colonial.html
http://www.ukans.edu/~ibetext/rev/index.html
Sections of the United States History Index, offering links to discovery and exploration, the colonial era, and the revolutionary era.

http://memory.loc.gov/ammem/ndlpedu/features/timeline/newnatn/newnatn.html
The New Nation, 1783–1815, a section of the Library of Congress's American Memory site, offering activities and resources.

http://memory.loc.gov/ammem/pihtml/pi001.html
Documents and images relating to George Washington's first inauguration, from "I Do Solemnly Swear...": Presidential Inaugurations, a Library of Congress site.

http://www.law.ou.edu/hist/
A site from the University of Oklahoma College of Law, offering the texts of many key historical documents, including early colonial charters, the Articles of Confederation of the United States of America, the *Federalist* papers, and the Northwest Ordinance.

In Print

Your local library will have many books on American history. The following is just a sampling of those relating to this volume.

Adams, James Truslow. *The Founding of New England*. Boston: Atlantic Monthly, 1923.

Andrews, Charles M. *The Colonial Period of American History*. New Haven: Yale, 1977.

Autobiography of Benjamin Franklin. Leonard W. Labaree, ed. New Haven: Yale, 1964.

Flexner, John Thomas. *George Washington*, 4 vols. Boston: Little, Brown, 1965–1972.

Hawke, David Freeman. *Paine*. New York: Norton, 1992.

Hostetler, John A. *The Amish*. Baltimore: Johns Hopkins, 1963.

Klees, Frederic. *The Pennsylvania Dutch*. New York: Macmillan, 1950.

Middlehoff, Robert. *The American Revolution*. New York: Oxford, 1982.

Morison, Samuel Eliot. *The European Discovery of America: The Northern Voyages*. New York: Oxford, 1971.

Schwartz, Bernard. *The Great Rights of Mankind: A History of the American Bill of Rights*. Madison: Madison House, 1992.

Wood, Gordon S. *The Creation of the American Republic 1776-1787*. New York: Norton, 1972.

Wright, Esmond. *Franklin of Philadelphia*. Cambridge: Harvard, 1988.

Note: For other general Internet sites and books, see Vol. 10, starting on p. 82.

Master Index

This Master Index covers all 10 volumes of *The Young Nation* and is repeated at the end of each volume. **Note:** Figures in bold are the volume numbers; the other figures give the page numbers.